CATHOLIC TRADITIONS AND TREASURES

Catholic
TRADITIONS
&TREASURES

An Illustrated Encyclopedia

HELEN HOFFNER, ED.D.

ILLUSTRATIONS BY DEIRDRE FOLLEY

SOPHIA INSTITUTE PRESS

MANCHESTER, NEW HAMPSHIRE

Sophia Institute Press
Box 5284, Manchester, NH 03108
1-800-888-9344

www.SophiaInstitute.com

Sophia Institute Press® is a registered trademark of Sophia Institute.

Library of Congress Cataloging-in-Publication Data

Names: Hoffner, Helen, 1958- author.
Title: Catholic traditions and treasures : an illustrated encyclopedia /
   Helen Hoffner, Ed.D.
Description: Manchester, New Hampshire : Sophia Institute Press, 2018. |
   Includes bibliographical references.
Identifiers: LCCN 2017059444 | ISBN 9781622824847 (hardcover : alk. paper)
Subjects: LCSH: Catholic Church—Customs and practices—Encyclopedias. |
   Religious articles—Encyclopedias.
Classification: LCC BX1754 .H59 2018 | DDC 282—dc23 LC record available at https://lccn.loc.gov/2017059444

6th printing

To my mother, Gloria Brady Hoffner,
who raised our family in a home filled with
Catholic treasures and traditions.

To the unknown artists and craftsmen
of the Church's history.

CONTENTS

2. The Sacraments

3. The Church Year

4. Public Catholic Devotions

5. Private Catholic Devotions

6. Titles of Mary

7. Catholicism in the Home

9. What Catholics Wear

10. Religious Art

11. Catholic Books You Need to Know

About the Author

CATHOLIC TRADITIONS AND TREASURES

INTRODUCTION

Many Catholics pray to St. Anthony when they lose something, and others keep a St. Christopher medal in their car. Many Catholics receive ashes on Ash Wednesday. Many such customs have been handed down in families, and sometimes Catholics continue to practice them without really thinking about them. Learning the history and significance of these customs, however, allows us to deepen our spiritual lives.

Religious artwork, medals, the colors and seasons of the Church year, and the many forms of public and private devotion are some of the treasures and traditions of our Catholic Faith. As with our family heirlooms, we should not only discover or rediscover the reasons behind them but also keep them always before us. In these pages, we will see how the treasures and traditions of our Faith remind us of our roots and also lead us toward our heavenly destination.

A statue of Mary on the lawn, a rosary hanging from a car's rearview mirror, and a holy-water font near the front door are outward signs of a Catholic lifestyle. Let us examine these and many other treasures and traditions and see how they can also form our inner lives.

Catholicism

The *Modern Catholic Dictionary* defines Catholicism as "the faith, ritual, and morals of the Roman Catholic Church as a historical reality, revealed in Jesus Christ and destined to endure until the end of time."[1] At the core of this system of doctrines and practices is the good news that Jesus, the Son of God, became man, was born of the Blessed Virgin Mary, died for the sins of mankind, and rose from the dead. The beliefs of the Catholic Faith are summarized in the Nicene Creed, a prayer that is said when Catholics gather for worship.

"This system of doctrine, cultus, and practice is called Catholic (universal) because it is intended for all mankind, for all time, contains all that is necessary, and is suitable in every circumstance of human life."[2] Catholicism spreads a message of hope in eternal life with God in heaven.

---

[1] "Catholicism," in Father John A. Hardon, S.J., *Modern Catholic Dictionary*, Real Presence Association, http://www.therealpresence.org/cgi-bin/getdefinition.pl.

[2] Ibid.

CHAPTER 1

THE CHURCH

The Catholic Church, also called the
Mystical Body of Christ, includes
members from all over the world.

The Catholic Hierarchy

The Church has a hierarchy of priests, bishops, and cardinals. The structure has served the Church well since the days of the apostles.

The Pope

The pope is the leader of the Catholic Church and the bishop of Rome. He is the successor of St. Peter, to whom Christ entrusted His Church. In addition to being a religious leader, the pope is recognized as a head of state because he leads the Vatican, which is an independent country.

The pope is required to meet with every Catholic bishop in the world at least once every five years to learn the conditions of their dioceses. This is an informative but potentially exhausting task. In 2016, for example, the Vatican's yearbook, *Annuario Pontificio*, reported that there were 5,237 Catholic bishops in the world. Consequently, the pope had to meet with approximately twenty bishops per week to fulfill his duty.

Cardinals

Cardinals advise and help the pope govern the Church. Because they serve in leadership roles around the world, cardinals can be the eyes and ears of the pope to alert him to problems as they arise. The pope personally selects each cardinal. The *Code of Canon Law* of 1917 requires that men must first be ordained priests before they can become cardinals. Since 1962, there has been a further stipulation that men must serve as bishops before they can become cardinals. Cardinals wear red robes. When a pope dies, the College of Cardinals elects his successor.

Bishops and Archbishops

Christ chose apostles to help in His work. Today's bishops are the successors of the apostles. Bishops govern dioceses (geographical groups of parishes) and serve in other administrative roles. The term *archbishop* is used for those who supervise other bishops and govern an archdiocese, an especially large diocese.

Bishops are selected in a secretive process that usually begins at the diocesan level and moves through a series of consultations. The names of priests who are strong candidates are sent to the pope, who makes the final decision.

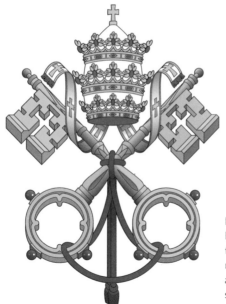

Papal seal (left): The keys, representing the keys to the kingdom of heaven, which Christ gave to St. Peter, are gold and silver, to symbolize the powers of loosing and binding (Matt. 16:19). The triple crown represents the pope's power as father of kings, governor of the world, and Vicar of Christ. The cross atop the globe surmounting the crown symbolizes the sovereignty of Christ.

A Catholic bishop, pope, and priest

Priests

What does a priest do? Pope Benedict XVI summed up the answer to that question when he told a crowd in St. Peter's Square that "the priest represents Christ."[1] The pope emphasized that the three duties of a priest are teaching, sanctifying, and governing. Priests celebrate Mass, administer sacraments, and serve as spiritual advisers. They also work as hospital, university, and military chaplains, teachers, missionaries, and administrators.

Deacons

Deacons are ordained ministers who may be transitional, if their ordination is a step on their path to the priesthood, or permanent, if they are not studying for the priesthood. Deacons do not say Mass, but they can baptize, read the Gospel, preach homilies, conduct funeral services, and, with permission, officiate at marriages held outside of a Mass. A married man can enter a program of studies to become a permanent deacon, but a deacon who is single cannot marry. If a married deacon is widowed, he may not remarry without special permission.

[1]   Benedict XVI, "The Priest's Three Duties," General Audience, April 14, 2010, http://www.ewtn.com/library/papaldoc/b16prduties.htm.

The Vatican, a Country That Leads a Church

The Vatican, home of the Catholic Church, is the world's smallest country. It comprises slightly more than one hundred acres and is one-eighth the size of New York City's Central Park. The Vatican is also one of the newest countries. Although popes have lived in the area since the fourth century, the Vatican has been recognized internationally as an independent sovereign state only since 1929. It has its own flag, coins, and postage stamps as well as license plates for the cars driven by its approximately eight hundred residents. The Vatican is a monarchy headed by the pope. Its governing body, the Holy See, carries out the administrative tasks of this country.

The Holy See

The Holy See, based in the Vatican, has been the governing body of the Catholic Church since early Christian times. It is a sovereign judicial entity led by the pope and recognized by international law. The Holy See maintains diplomatic relations with the United States and has an Apostolic Nunciature, the equivalent of an embassy, in Washington, D.C.

Often newspapers incorrectly report that decisions have been made by the Vatican. The term *Vatican*, however, refers only to a geographical area. The Holy See is the Church's decision-making body.

The Roman Curia

The Roman Curia is part of the Holy See, the governing body of the Church. It consists of offices that deal with a variety of essential tasks, including the supervision of Catholic education, the appointment of bishops, the pope's schedule, and channels of communication. Most of the employees of the Roman Curia are laypeople who go home each night to their families.

Papal Conclave

If the pope is the highest leader of the Church and answers only to God, how is he selected?

When a pope dies or resigns, the College of Cardinals takes responsibility for administrative duties until a new leader is selected.

Popes are chosen in an election process known as a papal conclave. All cardinals of the Church are invited to attend, but no more than 120 cardinals can vote, and those voting must be under the age of eighty. To give the cardinals of the world time to travel to the Vatican, papal conclaves do not begin until fifteen to twenty days after the death or resignation of a pope.

A papal conclave begins with Mass in St. Peter's Basilica in Rome. The cardinal electors (those eligible to vote) then go to the Sistine Chapel, take an oath of secrecy, and seal the doors for the first round of voting. Each cardinal writes his choice on a slip of paper, which is placed in a large chalice. There is always an overwhelming number of candidates because the new pope does not have to be chosen from among the cardinals. Any male who has been baptized in the Catholic Church is eligible, but since 1378, every pope has come from the College of Cardinals.

Typically, it takes one to seven days for the papal conclave to reach a decision. Each day, the cardinals participate in four rounds of voting until the field is narrowed and one candidate has received two-thirds of the votes.

St. Peter's Basilica in the Vatican

VATICAN II

On October 11, 1962, Pope John XXIII opened the Second Vatican Council, also known as Vatican II, whose greatest concern, he said, was "that the sacred deposit of Christian doctrine should be guarded and taught more efficaciously."[1] Pope John XXIII did not live to see the conclusion of the council, but his work was continued by his successor, Pope Paul VI. By the time Vatican II concluded on December 8, 1965, more than two thousand bishops from 116 countries had participated, and 16 documents were produced to explain and renew practices of the Church. Among the changes were that the Mass could be said in the vernacular rather than in Latin, Sunday Masses would have three Bible readings rather than two, and priests could face the congregation during Mass. Lay Catholics became more active in the Mass due to the recommendations of Vatican II.

As each round of votes is counted, the ballots on which the cardinals wrote their choices are destroyed. Ballots from the early rounds in which no candidate reached two-thirds of the vote are burned in a way that creates black smoke. When a candidate emerges with two-thirds of the vote, the ballots are treated with chemicals so that white smoke will rise when they are burned. Crowds gather in St. Peter's Square to watch the smoke rise each day. Black smoke means there has been no decision. When white smoke appears, there are shouts of joy as the world celebrates the election of a new pope.

There are no term limits for the papacy. A pope usually remains in office until death. Because resignations are rare, the world was stunned when Pope Benedict XVI stepped down in 2013. A pope had not resigned since Gregory XII in 1415.

---

[1] Floyd Anderson, ed., *Council Daybook: Vatican II, Sessions 1 and 2* (Washington: National Catholic Welfare Conference, 1965), 25.

Religious Orders

Some are called to serve the Church not in a particular diocese but in a religious order, which often has its own superiors, vows, work, and way of life.

Benedictines

There was perhaps no one more prepared to start a religious movement than St. Benedict, a man who was born into a wealthy family, moved into a cave to pray in solitude, and later transformed a chaotic monastery into a disciplined house of prayer. While living in the monastery at Monte Cassino, St. Benedict composed a guide to monastic life now known as the *Rule of St. Benedict*. Written circa 530, the *Rule of St. Benedict* has become widely used throughout the Western world.

Benedictines are monks and nuns who live according to the *Rule of St. Benedict*. Unlike many other religious orders, Benedictine monks and nuns do not have a central authority. Each Benedictine monastery is autonomous and answers only to the pope. The order's mottos is *Ora et labora* (pray and work).

Dominicans

In the thirteenth century, a young priest, Dominic de Guzman (1170–1221), later known as St. Dominic, was startled to learn that many people were unaware of the teachings of the Church. He decided to fix that problem by establishing an order of informed preachers to educate people and combat heresies. St. Dominic called his group the Order of Preachers, but they have become better known as the Dominicans. The Dominican Order has many branches and includes brothers, priests, nuns, and lay men and women among its members. They focus on prayer, study, and preaching and can often be found serving as teachers, parish priests, and hospital chaplains.

One of the most famous Dominicans is St. Thomas Aquinas (1225–1274). As a child he was educated at the Benedictine Abbey of Monte Cassino. When military conflicts forced Thomas to leave Monte Cassino briefly, however, the Dominican preacher John of St. Julian influenced him to join the newly founded Dominican Order rather than the Benedictines.

Franciscans

Sometimes religious orders that start with modest goals grow into worldwide movements. That happened when Francesco di Bernardone (1182–1226), later known as St. Francis of Assisi, asked Pope Innocent III for permission to start a religious order. St. Francis lived as a hermit and prayed in solitude. Others, however, admired his example, sought his guidance, and joined him in prayer. The result was the birth of a religious order known as the Franciscans.

Dominican friar

Franciscan friar

Today's Franciscan religious organization is composed of three orders, some with even more subdivisions. The first order of St. Francis is composed of priests and lay brothers. The second is composed of cloistered nuns known as the Order of St. Clare, or the Poor Clares. Males and females, religious and laypeople participate in the third order, living the Franciscan way in their owns states of life. All members of these three orders are known as Franciscans.

Although prayer is their priority, Franciscans have stepped up to take actions that have influenced history. In 1534, St. Thomas More (1478–1535), a member of the third order of the Franciscans, caused division in England when he refused to agree that King Henry VIII, rather than the pope, should lead the Church. In 1749, St. Junipero Serra (1713–1784) left a comfortable life as a Franciscan university professor and embarked on a rugged journey to establish missions throughout California. St. Marianne Cope (1838–1918), also known as Mother Marianne of Molokai, a member of the Third Order Regular of St. Francis, helped establish the first two Catholic hospitals in central New York. When other religious orders were hesitant to work with lepers in Hawaii, St. Marianne Cope volunteered for the job in 1883, and she fought with government and hospital officials to get the best possible care for the sick and dying.

Jesuits

Established in 1540 by St. Ignatius of Loyola, the Society of Jesus, better known as the Jesuits, is the largest religious order of priests and brothers in the Catholic Church.[2]

Jesuits are known for the establishment of prestigious universities such as Georgetown and Fordham, but they also serve in refugee camps and hospitals. They have been called God's marines because they complete missions for the Church in every part of the world and because their founder, St. Ignatius of Loyola, had distinguished military service.

Jesuits are instructed not to seek high offices in the Church but to serve wherever they are called. This guiding principle was put to the test in 2013, when, for the first time in history, a Jesuit, Cardinal Jorge M. Bergoglio, was chosen to become pope. He took the name Francis. In the Jesuit tradition, Pope Francis did not actively seek this leadership role, but he accepted the responsibility as the will of God.

Carmelites

The Carmelites take their name from their place of origin, Mount Carmel, the site in Palestine where the prophet Elijah prayed. Circa 1191, a group of pilgrims traveled from Europe to Mount Carmel to follow Elijah's example and live as hermits in the land of Jesus. By 1247, their order was approved by Pope Innocent IV.

The Carmelite order has branches that include priests, friars, nuns, and lay men and women. They have been called the white friars because they often wear a white habit for special occasions and are buried in a white habit.

Some notable Carmelites are St. John of the Cross, St. Simon Stock, St. Teresa of Avila, St. Thérèse of Lisieux, St. Teresa Benedicta of the

---

[2] "About Us," website of the Jesuit Order, http://jesuits.org/aboutus.

Cross, St. Elizabeth of the Trinity, and Lucia dos Santos (1907–2005).

Trappists

Anyone seeking an especially disciplined order might consider joining the Cistercians of the Strict Observance, better known as the Trappists.

Many early religious orders followed the guide to monastic living written by St. Benedict. Over time, however, some relaxed their guidelines and adopted practices that did not follow every rule exactly as written.

In 1098, the Order of Cistercians was started to promote a stricter way of life than the one that the Benedictines of that time followed. When the Abbot of La Trappe wanted even tougher rules in 1656, the name Trappists became used for groups that strictly observe the Rule of St. Benedict.

Today's Trappist monasteries are composed of sisters and monks living in self-sufficient communities. They fill their days by praying and producing goods to sustain their communities.

Trappist monasteries make many items to sell, but they have become known for their beer. The early monasteries followed Jesus' example of offering food and drink to weary travelers. Often the monks could not give their guests water because the nearby rivers carried diseases. Consequently, monks brewed beer as a way of sanitizing and adding nutrients to the water. The monks began to sell their beer to raise funds to sustain their monasteries.

As the monks' beer gained popularity, many commercial breweries with no ties to religious organizations began to call their products Trappist beers. To stop misuse, the Trappists were forced to protect their name by taking legal action in 1962. In 1997, Trappist monasteries in Belgium, the Netherlands, and Germany formed the International Trappist Association (ITA). The ITA guidelines state that their logo can be used only on beer and other products made in a monastery with the supervision of monks.

The 2011 film *Of Gods and Men* offered a rare glimpse into the lives of Trappist monks in Algeria in the 1990s. The film showed that although Trappists live in quiet monasteries, they do not turn their backs on the suffering of the outside world.

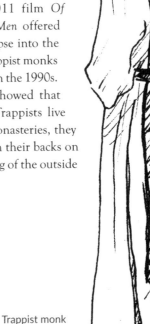

Trappist monk

CHAPTER 2

THE SACRAMENTS

The *Catechism of the Catholic Church* tells us, "The seven sacraments touch all the stages and all the important moments of Christian life: they give birth and increase, healing and mission to the Christian's life of faith" (1210).

The Seven Sacraments

A sacrament is an outward sign instituted by Christ to give grace. The seven sacraments of the Catholic Church are Baptism, Penance, Holy Eucharist, Confirmation, Holy Orders, Matrimony, and Anointing of the Sick. Baptism, Confirmation, and the Eucharist are the Sacraments of Initiation, and they "lay the foundations of every Christian life" (CCC 1212). For most Catholics, these sacraments are received during childhood. Those who enter the Church as adults often receive these sacraments at the Easter Vigil Mass, after a period of study and preparation. The *Catechism* calls Penance and Anointing of the Sick the Sacraments of Healing, and Holy Orders and Matrimony the Sacraments at the Service of Communion.

Baptism

Baptism is the first sacrament a person receives, and it enables him to receive other sacraments. Through Baptism, Original Sin is washed away, and the baptized person receives sanctifying grace, by which he becomes a member of the Church, a child of God, and an heir of heaven. The baptized person receives an indelible spiritual mark, a sign of his belonging to Christ.

Baptismal font in the Baptistry of San Giovanni, Florence, Italy

In the Catholic Church, Baptism usually occurs in infancy. For his Baptism, a baby usually wears a white garment, often a gown made of satin. The white garment symbolizes that the child has put on Christ. A candle is lit from the Paschal candle, showing that, by Baptism, Christ has enlightened the child.

The baptismal certificate is the passport to all things Catholic. A person must show it as proof of being Catholic when he wishes to be married in a Catholic church or serve as a godparent.

Confirmation

In the United States, it was long customary for Confirmation candidates to select a new name, usually the name of a saint who could serve as a role model. Many dioceses have stopped the practice of taking Confirmation names in order to emphasize the link between Baptism, Confirmation, and the Eucharist.

The effects of Confirmation are an increase in grace, a strengthening of faith and of the gifts of the Holy Spirit (fear of the Lord, piety, knowledge, fortitude, counsel, understanding, and wisdom), and an indelible spiritual mark, which "is the sign that Jesus Christ has marked a Christian with the seal of his Spirit" (CCC 1304). The sacrament is usually administered by a bishop, and the rite includes the anointing of the confirmand's forehead with holy oil (chrism) and the laying on of hands.

The Eucharist

Pope John Paul II said, "The Eucharist 'contains the Church's entire spiritual wealth, that is, Christ himself, our Passover and living bread, who, through His very flesh, made vital and vitalizing by the Holy Spirit, offers life' to the human family. This is the heart of the Church's life, and also of the consecrated life."[1]

The *Modern Catholic Dictionary* defines the Eucharist as "the true Body and Blood of Jesus Christ, who is really and substantially present under the appearances of bread and wine, in order to offer himself in the sacrifice of the Mass and to be received as spiritual food in Holy Communion."[2] During the Mass, through the ministry of the priest, bread and wine are transformed in substance into the Body and Blood, Soul and Divinity of Christ while retaining their taste, smell, texture, and so forth. The Eucharist is one of the sacraments that Catholics receive most frequently, in Holy Communion. Children usually receive their First Holy Communion, around the age of seven.

First Holy Communion

One of the biggest celebrations for Catholic families occurs on a child's First Holy Communion day. Although First Holy Communion is usually considered a children's event,

TABERNACLE

Every Catholic church has a tabernacle, a place where the Blessed Sacrament is reserved. In most churches, the tabernacle rests in a place of honor behind the altar so that it is visible to the faithful and easily accessible to the priest. Canon law 938 states, "The tabernacle in which the Eucharist is regularly reserved is to be immovable, made of solid or opaque material, and locked so that the danger of profanation may be entirely avoided."

According to the *General Instruction of the Roman Missal* (233), one should genuflect whenever passing in front of the Blessed Sacrament reposed in the tabernacle.

[1] John Paul II, Post-Synodal Apostolic Exhortation *Vita Consecrata* (March 25, 1996), no. 95, http://w2.vatican.va/content/john-paul-ii/en/apost_exhortations/documents/hf_jp-ii_exh_25031996_vita-consecrata.html.

[2] "Eucharist," in Father John A. Hardon, S.J., *Modern Catholic Dictionary*, Real Presence Association, http://www.therealpresence.org/cgi-bin/getdefinition.pl.

it has been so only since 1910. On August 15 of that year, Pope Pius X issued a decree reestablishing *Quam Singulari*, an ancient Church law on First Communion. This decree lowered the age for first reception of Communion from fourteen to seven, the age at which the Church considers children to understand right and wrong. Pope Pius X opened his remarks on this issue with the biblical quote "Let the children come to me, and do not hinder them; for to such belongs the kingdom of heaven" (Matt. 19:14).

First Holy Communion Attire

There are many customs related to the clothes children wear for their First Holy Communion. Boys typically wear a white suit or a blue suit with a white tie. A gold chalice pin may be worn on the tie. For girls, First Holy Communion is an occasion to wear a beautiful white dress and veil. Some families use fabric from the mother's wedding gown to create a dress that is passed down from sister to sister. To keep a reverent focus, a Spanish custom uses First Holy Communion as an opportunity to encourage charity. Rather than spending great sums on a suit or a dress, wealthy families buy less extravagant clothing and use the money they save to purchase an outfit for a child in the First Communion class who cannot afford new attire.

White clothing for First Holy Communion is a custom that has a spiritual basis. In his address to the International Congress of Master Tailors and Designers on September 10, 1954, Pope Pius XII stated, "The white garment of a child on the morning of his First Communion, that of a young woman on the day of her marriage: do these not symbolize the totally immaterial splendor of a soul which is offering the best of itself?"[3]

FIRST HOLY COMMUNION MEMENTOES

"In remembrance of my First Holy Communion": those words have graced certificates given to children around the world on their First Holy Communion day. The certificates of the 1950s to 1960s had elaborate inserts with brocade fabric and gold crucifixes. Their beauty added to the reverence of the event and inspired the children receiving them.

After a First Holy Communion, there is often a party with a beautiful cake taking center stage. The classic First Holy Communion cake topper shows Christ standing at an altar rail wearing a red robe as He holds a chalice and a Communion Host. The figure is available with either a boy or a girl kneeling at the altar. Hartland Plastics began making this cake topper in 1959, and it has remained in use. The scene is dated, however, because since the new Mass of Pope Paul VI in 1969, Catholics usually stand when receiving Communion. Many churches have removed the altar rails at which communicants once knelt.

---

[3] Kay Toy Fenner, *American Catholic Etiquette* (Westminster, MD: Newman Press, 1961), 26.

Penance

On the evening of the first Easter, Jesus said to His apostles "If you forgive the sins of any, they are forgiven; if you retain the sins of any, they are retained" (John 20:22–23). Jesus gave priests the authority to forgive sins in His name. Priests exercise this authority in the sacrament of Penance, also known as Confession or Reconciliation, in which the faithful confess their sins and receive forgiveness.

Canon law requires Catholics to make a confession at least once a year, but the Church encourages the practice of frequent confession. Penitents may confess their sins to a priest while kneeling behind a screen or grille or while sitting face-to-face with the priest.

A confessional

Anointing of the Sick

Prior to Vatican II in the 1960s, this sacrament was called Extreme Unction (final anointing), but it is now known as Anointing of the Sick, as it may be received not only by those near death but also by those facing surgery or dealing with serious illness. Through anointing and the prayers of the priest, this sacrament gives strength to the soul and sometimes to the body.

Catholic homes often contain a sick-call crucifix set that is used when a priest comes to visit the seriously ill. The front of the crucifix slides open to reveal a compartment containing two blessed candles and a vial of holy water. Because a priest usually brings the Blessed Sacrament on sick calls, custom dictates that a family member carrying a lit blessed candle should meet him at the door and escort him to the sick person's room.

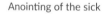

Anointing of the sick

Holy Orders

All members of the Catholic Church receive the sacrament of Baptism, and most also receive Holy Communion and Confirmation. Very few, however, receive the sacrament of Holy Orders, which ordains men to the priesthood. There is only one sacrament of Holy Orders but men can be ordained at three levels: the diaconate (deacons), the presbyterate (priests), and the episcopate (bishops).

Matrimony

Matrimony is the sacrament that unites a man and a woman in marriage. "On the threshold of his public life Jesus performs his first sign—at his mother's request—during a wedding feast (John 2:1–11). The Church attaches great importance to Jesus' presence at the wedding at Cana. She sees in it the confirmation of the goodness of marriage and the proclamation that thenceforth marriage will be an efficacious sign of Christ's presence" (CCC 1613). The ministers of the sacrament of Matrimony are the bride and groom, who confer the sacrament on each other. Usually Catholic weddings take place in the home parish of the bride, although canon law allows alternate venues. Canon 1115 states, "Marriages are to be celebrated in a parish where either of the contracting parties has a domicile, quasidomicile, or month-long residence or, if it concerns transients, in the parish where they actually reside. With the permission of the proper ordinary or proper pastor, marriages can be celebrated elsewhere."

WEDDING ROSARIES

As she walks down the aisle, the Catholic bride may carry a rosary in addition to her bouquet of flowers. Often the rosary is a family heirloom with pearl or crystal beads. Most brides carry the traditional five-decade Dominican rosary; some carry a Lasso or Mexican Lasso Rosary.

The Lasso Rosary consists of two traditional five-decade rosaries that are linked together at the center medal. During the wedding ceremony, the priest places one part around the neck of the groom and the other around the neck of the bride. Prayers are then offered for the couple. After the ceremony, the priest removes the Lasso Rosary and gives it to the couple to hang in their home.

Another version is the Mexican Lasso Rosary, which is made up of three five-decade rosaries. When the Mexican Lasso Rosary is used, one part is placed around the neck of the groom and one around the neck of the bride. The third section hangs between the couple. During the wedding reception, the bride takes the Mexican Lasso Rosary apart and gives one section to her mother and one to the groom's mother and asks the families to pray for the couple. The bride and groom keep the third section to hang in their home.

CHAPTER 3

THE CHURCH YEAR

What are the seasons of the year? Most people will answer winter, spring, summer, and fall. Catholics, however, may respond with the seasons of the Church year, known officially as the liturgical year.

Liturgical Seasons

The General Roman Calendar divides the liturgical year into six seasons: Advent, Christmas, Lent, the Sacred Triduum, Easter, and Ordinary Time. Many of the Church's feast days occur on fixed dates, such as the celebration of Christmas on December 25. Movable feasts, such as Easter, are celebrated on different dates each year and those dates may not be the same in every country.

Advent

While most of the world begins a new year on January 1, the Catholic Church begins her new liturgical year in late November or early December with the season of Advent, a time of preparation for the coming of Christ at Christmas and for His Second Coming at the end of time.

Traditional Advent customs include lighting the candles of an Advent wreath and opening the doors of an Advent calendar.

Christmas

Christmas celebrates the birth of Jesus Christ. The Christmas season begins on the evening of December 24 and ends on the feast of the Baptism of Our Lord, usually between January 9 and 13.

During the Christmas season, many Catholics enjoy singing carols during Mass, with their families, and sometimes in public settings. Children sing many of these carols during Christmas pageants, in which they reenact the story of Christ's birth.

St. Francis of Assisi began the tradition of building manger scenes, which are common in Catholic Christmas celebrations.

Lent

Lent begins on Ash Wednesday and ends on the evening of Holy Thursday. It is a time in which Catholics make sacrifices and perform charitable works as penance for sin. Catholics between eighteen and fifty-nine are required to fast on Ash Wednesday and on Good Friday, and Catholics over fourteen are required to abstain from meat on Fridays during Lent (see "Fasting" and "Friday Abstinence" in chapter 5).

The Catholic Church refers to Lent as an observance of forty days. Counting these days, however, can be confusing because Sundays are not included in the tally. Catholics are not required to fast and do penance on Sundays.

The Sacred Triduum

The holiest days of the Church year are called the Triduum (meaning "three days"), which extends from the evening of Holy Thursday to the evening of Easter Sunday.

Holy Thursday

Holy Thursday, celebrated on the Thursday evening before Easter, commemorates the Last Supper, the event at which Christ instituted the sacraments of Holy Eucharist and Holy Orders.

Holy Thursday is also known as Maundy Thursday. The word *Maundy* comes from the Latin word *mandatum*, which means "mandate." It was on Holy Thursday that Christ gave His followers the mandate "Love one another; even as I have loved you" (John 13:34–35).

Every Mass is a reenactment of the Last Supper, the final meal that Jesus celebrated with His apostles. Holy Thursday, however, honors the Last Supper in a special way. Often churches invite members of the parish to have their feet washed by the priest. This is done because Christ washed the feet of the apostles as an example of humility and service to others.

LITURGICAL COLORS

From the red and green decorations of Christmas to pink balloons for a baby girl, colors have been associated with special meanings. The Catholic Church likewise uses certain colors for liturgical events and seasons:

- **White** symbolizes rejoicing and purity of soul. White vestments are worn during the Christmas and Easter seasons (except on the feasts of martyrs), for feasts of our Lord (except those of His Passion), the Blessed Virgin Mary, angels, and saints who were not martyrs.

- **Red** is a reminder of the blood of Christ and of martyrdom, so red vestments are worn on Palm Sunday, on Good Friday, and on the feasts of martyrs. Because red also symbolizes the fire of God's love, the Holy Spirit, it is worn on Pentecost and often for Confirmations.

- **Purple** is a sign of penance, sacrifice, and preparation and is worn during the seasons of Advent and Lent.

- **Green** is a reminder of spring and new life, and thus is a sign of hope and growth. The Church uses green during most of Ordinary Time.

- **Blue** is associated with Mary, the Mother of God. Blue vestments are worn on Marian feast days, and blue ribbons and blue garments are often worn during May processions honoring Mary.

Good Friday

Because Good Friday honors the day on which Christ died on the Cross, it is especially somber. Church bells do not ring, and statues and other adornments in the church are covered. The hours between noon and three o'clock are passed quietly with special reverence in remembrance of the hours when Christ hung on the Cross. No Masses are said on Good Friday, but Holy Communion, consecrated on Holy Thursday, may be distributed during the Good Friday liturgy. Fasting is required on Good Friday for Catholics between eighteen and fifty-nine who are in good health.

Holy Saturday

Holy Saturday, the day before Easter, is a time to reflect upon Christ's suffering and death on the Cross. No Masses are said until the evening, and only the sacraments of Penance and the Anointing of the Sick can be administered. Communion may be given to sick and the dying.

On the evening of Holy Saturday, the Easter Vigil is celebrated, beginning with the lighting of a bonfire outside the church. A new Paschal candle, which symbolizes the light of Christ and is used throughout the Easter season, is lit from this fire, and the celebrant and the faithful process into the church. Nine readings are provided for the Mass: seven from the Old Testament and two from the New. The faithful renew their baptismal promises, and new members are welcomed into the Church through Baptism. Some may also receive Confirmation.

Easter

Easter, the greatest feast of the Church, is the celebration of Christ's Resurrection from the dead. After the forty days of preparation for Easter during

The inscription "Jesus of Nazareth, King of the Jews" was put on Jesus' Cross during his Crucifixion (John 19:19). Many crucifixes therefore bear the inscription "INRI," an acronym for the Latin version: *Iesus Nazarenus Rex Iudaeorum.*

Lent, the Easter season is celebrated for fifty days, culminating with the feast of Pentecost.

Ordinary Time

Although every day has its special moments, the Catholic Church designates two periods each year as Ordinary Time. The first starts on the feast of the Baptism of Our Lord (usually celebrated in early January) and ends on the day before Ash Wednesday. The second period of Ordinary Time begins on the Monday after Pentecost Sunday (the last day of the Easter Season) and ends on the Saturday before the first Sunday of Advent (in late November or early December). It is called Ordinary Time because the weeks are ordered, or numbered.

Ordinary Time is a time for Catholics to grow in faith as they reflect on Christ's life, miracles, and teachings in light of the Resurrection.

Feast Days

Feast days are days set aside each year to honor Mary, the saints, and mysteries of the Faith.

Types of Feast Days

Memorials

In the hierarchy of feast days, memorials hold the lowest status. Memorials can be obligatory and optional. Obligatory memorials recognize a saint or an attribute of Jesus or Mary, such as the Immaculate Heart of Mary. Optional memorials can honor saints.

Feasts

Of mid-level importance in the calendar are feasts—days on which Catholics remember saints as well as titles and mysteries of Jesus and Mary.

Solemnities

Solemnities are the highest designation of feast days, and some, such as the Assumption of the Blessed Virgin Mary on August 15 and All Saints' Day on November 1, are holy days of obligation, on which Catholics are required to attend Mass. Only the most significant mysteries of the Faith, such as the Resurrection, or the feast days of saints who influenced salvation history, such as St. John the Baptist, are considered solemnities.

Holy Days of Obligation

Catholics must attend Mass on Sundays or on Saturday evenings (the Sunday vigil) and on designated holy days of obligation. These holy days are not the same throughout the world but are set by local governing bodies. For example, the U.S. Conference of Catholic Bishops declared the following dates to be holy days of obligation in the United States:

- **January 1:** Solemnity of Mary, the Mother of God
- **Thursday of the Sixth Week of the Easter Season:** Ascension Thursday
- **August 15:** Solemnity of the Assumption of the Blessed Virgin Mary
- **November 1:** Solemnity of All Saints
- **December 8:** Solemnity of the Immaculate Conception
- **December 25:** Solemnity of the Birth of Jesus Christ

Major Feast Days

Christmas Day

Christmas is the celebration of the birth, or nativity, of Jesus Christ. It is a feast full of joy. In a Nativity sermon, St. John Chrysostom (347–407) said, "All join to praise this holy feast, beholding the Godhead here on earth and man in heaven. He Who is above now for our redemption dwells here below, and we who are lowly are by divine mercy raised up."

Midnight Mass is one of the most beautiful and well-known Christmas traditions of the Catholic Church. The faithful gather in the darkness of midnight to celebrate the birth of the One who brought light to the world. Many churches begin and end Midnight Mass with candlelit processions.

Candlemas

Candlemas, observed on February 2, celebrates the day on which Joseph and Mary presented their newborn Son, Jesus, in the Temple. Candles are associated with this event because it was on this day that Simeon, a devout man in the Temple, took the baby Jesus in his arms and declared Him to be "a light for revelation to the Gentiles, and for glory to thy people, Israel" (Luke 2:32). Many churches celebrate Candlemas with candlelight processions during Mass and bless candles for the faithful to use at home.

ASH WEDNESDAY

Ash Wednesday marks the beginning of Lent. During Mass on Ash Wednesday, persons who present themselves receive ashes on their forehead. The ashes symbolize the dust from which God made us and recall the ancient Jewish tradition of penance. As the priest speaks the words "Remember that you are dust, and to dust you shall return," he traces a cross on the forehead of the penitent with ashes.

Ash Wednesday

Ash Wednesday is the first day of Lent. On this day, priests or their designees use ashes to make a small cross on the foreheads of Church members. This is a reminder that we must all die and face God in judgment.

Palms, which Catholics use to celebrate Palm Sunday, are burned to create the ashes used on the following Ash Wednesday.

Catholics are encouraged but not required to receive ashes. Ashes can be distributed during a Mass, or a priest or his designee may bring ashes to schools, hospitals, offices, and other appropriate gathering places.

Ash Wednesday is not a holy day of obligation, but Catholics between eighteen and fifty-nine are required to fast on that day (see "Fasting" in chapter 5).

Palm Sunday

The Sunday before Easter is called Palm Sunday. It recalls the day on which Christ entered Jerusalem to the cheers of a joyful crowd waving palm branches to signify victory. It is the first day of Holy Week, the week before Easter.

On Palm Sunday, Catholic churches distribute palms, which are blessed by a priest. Catholics keep the blessed palms in their homes as a reminder of Christ's victory.

Traditionally, Catholics have placed palms behind crucifixes and religious pictures in their homes or on the graves of family members. Many weave the palms to make crosses.

Because palms distributed in churches have been blessed, they should never be discarded as trash. Palms that have become dry and brittle should be returned to a church so that they can be burned to create the ashes used on Ash Wednesday of the following year.

Easter Sunday

When Christ rose from the dead, He brought new life to the Church. Catholics often wear new clothes to church on Easter Sunday to show that Christ has given them new life. Easter is celebrated for eight days. On each day, the faithful hear accounts of the Resurrection in the Gospel at Mass. The eighth day, or octave day, of Easter is Divine Mercy Sunday.

Pentecost

Pentecost is the observance of the day on which the Holy Spirit came to the apostles and gave them the strength to preach Christ's words. The name *Pentecost* comes from the Greek word for fifty. It is a movable feast that is celebrated fifty days after Easter. Pentecost usually falls between May 10 and June 13. It is the last day of the Easter season.

Pentecost is called the birthday of the Church:

> "On the day of Pentecost,... the Church was publicly displayed to the multitude, the Gospel began to spread among the nations by means of preaching, and there was presaged that union of all peoples in the catholicity of the faith by means of the Church of the new covenant."[1]
> ... The Church, which had just been born in this way on the day of Pentecost by the work of the Holy Spirit, was immediately revealed to the world.[2]

THE DATE OF EASTER

Christmas is celebrated on December 25. When is Easter? That depends on the calendar you follow and the phases of the moon. The Roman Catholic Church follows the Gregorian calendar and observes Easter on the first Sunday after the first full moon on or after March 21. Roman Catholics always celebrate Easter on a Sunday between March 21 and April 25.

The Risen Christ is often symbolized by a lamb with a flag.

---

[1] Second Vatican Council, Decree *Ad Gentes* on the Missionary Activity of the Church, no. 4.

[2] John Paul II, General Audience, October 2, 1991, nos. 4–5.

Feast of the Sacred Heart

The heart is the universal symbol of love. Pope Pius XII explained the concept of the Sacred Heart by saying, "Devotion to the Sacred Heart of Jesus, of its very nature, is a worship of the love with which God, through Jesus, loved us, and at the same time, an exercise of our own love by which we are related to God and to other men."[3]

In 1765, Pope Clement XIII officially recognized and approved devotion to the Sacred Heart. On August 23, 1856, Pope Pius IX declared that a worldwide feast day would be devoted to the Sacred Heart. The feast of the Sacred Heart of Jesus is celebrated each year on the Friday following the second Sunday after Pentecost, or nineteen days after Pentecost.

All Saints' Day

All Saints' Day, a solemnity and holy day of obligation in most countries, is celebrated on November 1. The vigil of this solemnity is All Hallow's Eve, or Halloween.

Circa 1261, the Church began the practice of setting aside one day each year to honor all saints, those who were well known as well as those who may not have received recognition. Originally, only people who had been martyred were recognized. Later, individuals who lived extraordinary lives of holiness were added.

There are not enough days in the year to give every saint his own feast day, so all saints are honored on November 1.

Catholics are encouraged to follow the examples set by the saints. In his 2013 All Saints' Day address, Pope Francis said, "To be a saint is not a privilege of a few.... All of us in baptism have the inheritance of being able to become saints."[4]

All Souls' Day

When loved ones die, Catholics pray that their souls will be received into heaven. Circa 1030, St. Odilo proposed a day to pray specifically for the dead.

Odilo was the abbot of the monastery of Cluny, France. Saddened that many young men had been killed in war, he told all members of his monastery to spend a full day praying for the souls of the deceased. Other monasteries followed his example and began to observe a day for all souls. Eventually, the commemoration of All Souls' Day was added to the calendar of the Catholic Church. All Souls' Day is celebrated on November 2.

Solemnity of Christ the King

The solemnity of Christ the King was instituted in 1925 by Pope Pius XI, who felt that world leaders leaned toward secularism and did not recognize Christ's authority. This feast, classified as a solemnity, was originally celebrated on the Sunday before All Saints' Day. In 1969, Pope Paul VI moved the observance to the Sunday before the first Sunday of Advent because he believed that this feast deserved a more prominent place on the liturgical calendar.

Christ the King

---

3   Pius XII, Encyclical *Haurietis Aquas* (May 15, 1956), no. 107.

4   Catholic News Agency/EWTN News, "Pope Francis: Sanctity Is for Everyone, Saints Are Not Supermen," Catholic News Agency, November 1, 2013, http://www.catholicnewsagency.com/news/pope-francis-sanctity-is-for-everyone-saints-are-not-supermen/.

Marian Months

The Church dedicates the months of May and October to the Blessed Virgin Mary.

May, the Month of Mary

In May, flowers bloom abundantly and spring returns to many parts of the earth. In this month, said Pope Paul VI, "Christians, in their churches and their homes, offer the Virgin Mother more fervent and loving acts of homage and veneration; and it is the month in which a greater abundance of God's merciful gifts comes down to us from our Mother's throne."[5]

It was on May 13, 1917, that Mary made the first of her many appearances to three children in Fatima, Portugal. The feasts of the Visitation and of Our Lady, Queen of the Apostles are also usually celebrated in May. One of the greatest Marian traditions is the May procession.

October, the Month of the Rosary

October is the month of the Rosary and is also a time to remember Marian events. Pope Pius V urged all Catholics to pray the Rosary for the Christians' victory over the Turks in the Battle of Lepanto, on October 7, 1571. When their prayers were answered, the pope decreed that October 7 would henceforth be commemorated as the feast of Our Lady of Victory. In 1573, Pope Gregory XIII changed the name of the feast to Our Lady of the Rosary.

More than three hundred years later, Mary appeared in Fatima, Portugal, and said, "I am the

MAY PROCESSIONS AND THE CROWNING OF MARY

Of all the ceremonies of the Catholic Church, May processions tend to evoke the most vivid memories.

Since medieval times, the month of May has been associated with Mary, the Mother of Jesus. May processions honoring Mary have been popular in the United States since before Vatican II.

Typically, children walk in a procession from their Catholic school to the local church while singing hymns to Mary. A girl who has been selected to be the May queen walks at the end of the line. When the group arrives in the church, the May queen places a crown of flowers upon a statue of Mary.

Families often place a statue of Mary in their homes and have their own May crownings.

[5] Paul VI, Encyclical *Mense Maio* (April 29, 1965), no. 1.

Lady of the Rosary."[6] The crowd that gathered that day, October 13, 1917, witnessed an event known as the Miracle of the Sun (see "Our Lady of the Rosary/Our Lady of Fatima" in chapter 6).

Mary, our Mother, is honored every day, but the months of May and October give Catholics special opportunities to reflect upon her role in the life of the Church.

October is the month of the Rosary in memory of Our Lady's intercession at the Battle of Lepanto on October 7, 1571, and her miracle at Fatima on October 13, 1917.

6   John Haffert, "The Message of Fatima in Our Lady's Own Words," International Pilgrim Virgin Statue Foundation, http://www.pilgrimvirginstatue.com/message-of-fatima.

CHAPTER 4

PUBLIC CATHOLIC DEVOTIONS

The Church recognizes that the spiritual life is not limited to participation in the Mass. St. Paul tells us to "pray constantly" (1 Thess. 5:17), and public devotional practices help us to do this.

Outward Signs of the Faith

Catholic worship involves not only the mind and the heart but the whole person. Our bearing, the gestures we make, and the sacred items we use are meaningful in themselves and help to enhance our prayer. Here are some common examples.

The Sign of the Cross

You can identify the Catholics in a room by noticing those who make a gesture known as the Sign of the Cross before they pray. St. Francis de Sales explains:

> The Christian first lifts his hand toward his head while saying, "In the name of the Father," in order to show that the Father is the first person of the Blessed Trinity and the principal and origin of the others. Then, he moves his hand downward toward the stomach while saying, "and of the Son," in order to show that the Son proceeds from the Father, who sent Him here below into the Virgin's womb. Finally, he pulls his hand across from the left shoulder to the right while saying, "and of the Holy Spirit," in order to show that the Holy Spirit, being the third person of the Blessed Trinity, proceeds from the Father and from the Son and is their bond of love and charity, and that it is by His grace that we enjoy the effects of the Passion.
>
> When making the Sign of the Cross, therefore, we confess three great mysteries: the Trinity, the Passion, and the remission of sins.[1]

The Sign of the Cross has been used in prayer since the earliest days of the Church. Circa 386, St. Cyril of Jerusalem stated, "Be the cross our seal, made with boldness by our fingers on our brow and in everything; over the bread we eat and the cups we drink, in our comings and in our goings out; before our sleep, when we lie down and when we awake; when we are traveling, and when we are at rest."[2]

Genuflecting

To genuflect is to make a reverent acknowledgment by bending the right knee to the ground. Before entering a pew, when leaving a pew, or when passing in front of the tabernacle, Catholics genuflect toward the tabernacle to show respect and reverence for Christ's presence in the Blessed Sacrament.

Kneeling

During Mass and at other times of prayer, Catholics kneel to show reverence and humility before God. In Ephesians 3:14, St. Paul says, "For this reason I bow my knees before the Father."

When Catholics kneel to pray privately, they are following the example Jesus set on the night before His Crucifixion. The Gospel of St. Luke states that after asking the apostles to keep watch with Him, Christ "withdrew from them about a stone's throw, and knelt down and prayed" (Luke 22:41).

---

[1] St. Francis de Sales, *The Sign of the Cross: The Fifteen Most Powerful Words in the English Language*, ed. and trans. Christopher O. Blum (Manchester, NH: Sophia Institute Press, 2013), 9–10.

[2] *The Works of St. Cyril of Jerusalem*, vol. 2 (Washington, D.C.: Catholic University of Press, 1970).

The practice of kneeling during Mass has undergone many changes. Customs vary among countries. In 1969, for example, the U.S. Conference of Catholic Bishops decided that Catholics in the United States should kneel during the entire Eucharistic Prayer. In 1980, the Sacred Congregation for Sacraments and Divine Worship decreed that local authorities could decide whether Catholics should kneel or stand to receive Communion.

Whether one kneels or stands, a reverent attitude should be maintained for prayer.

Holy Oil

Throughout history, oil has been used to soothe burns, alleviate dry skin, and enrich foods. Oil has become associated with healing and beauty. The Catholic Church uses oil to signify healing and the gift of the Holy Spirit.

Catholics are anointed with oil when they receive the sacraments of Baptism, Confirmation, Holy Orders, and Anointing of the Sick. Each year during Holy Week, a bishop celebrates the Chrism Mass in the cathedral of his diocese. During this Mass, the bishop blesses the oil that the diocese will need for the year. There are three types of oil: the Oil of Catechumens (olive oil used for those preparing to enter the Church), the Oil of the Sick (olive oil used for Anointing of the Sick), and Chrism (olive oil mixed with balsam, used for Baptism, Confirmation, and Holy Orders). After the bishop has blessed the oil, it is distributed to parishes within the diocese and used when these sacraments are administered.

Incense

Incense is a gum or powder that produces a pleasant fragrance when burned. In ancient times, incense was burned to purify objects so that they could be offered as worthy sacrifices to God. Psalm 141:2 states, "Let my prayer be counted as incense before thee, and the lifting up of my hands as an evening sacrifice!" The Church uses incense as a reminder that our prayers rise toward heaven.

The use of incense at Mass is optional. Church guidelines allow incense to be used at specific times, including the entrance procession, the proclamation of the Gospel, the preparation of the gifts, and the elevation of the Body and Blood of Christ.

Incense is used during Benediction, the liturgical service during which the faithful adore the Blessed Sacrament displayed in a monstrance.

Incense can bring comfort to families attending the funeral Mass of a loved one. The priest incenses the coffin when it is brought into the church. As the smoke rises, the congregation is reminded of their hope that the soul of the deceased will rise to heaven to be reunited with God.

Blessing of Throats

The feast of St. Blaise is celebrated on February 3 with the blessing of throats. This is done to ask God to protect the faithful from diseases of the throat and other illnesses. The blessing can be given during or outside of Mass. A priest or deacon holds two crossed candles against the throat of each person as he invokes the blessing.

Why do Catholics turn to St. Blaise for relief from sore throats? According to legend, a mother approached St. Blaise and begged him to help her son, who had a fish bone lodged in his throat. Blaise prayed, and the bone was dislodged.

Prayers and Devotions

In addition to attending Mass, Catholics can participate in public devotions that focus on various aspects of the Faith, including Scripture, the Holy Eucharist, and Christ's Passion. Here are some examples.

The Ten Commandments

The Ten Commandments, given by God to Moses, show us how to lead moral lives. Pope St. John Paul II in his 1993 encyclical *Veritatis Splendor*, emphasized their importance by repeating the words of St. Thomas Aquinas, "The [ten] commandments contain the whole natural law."[3]

The Ten Commandments

(See Exod. 20:1–17.)

1. I am the LORD your God; you shall have no other gods before me.
2. You shall not take the name of the LORD your God in vain.
3. Remember the sabbath day, to keep it holy.
4. Honor your father and your mother.
5. You shall not kill.
6. You shall not commit adultery.
7. You shall not steal.
8. You shall not bear false witness against your neighbor.
9. You shall not covet your neighbor's wife.
10. You shall not covet your neighbor's goods.

Divine Office

The Divine Office, or Liturgy of the Hours, is the official prayer of the Church, prayed at certain hours of the day. It consists of prayers, biblical readings, and psalms said at sunrise (Lauds), dusk (Vespers), and at other specific hours. Members of the clergy and of religious orders pray the Divine Office daily. Laypersons are also encouraged to do

---

[3]   John Paul II, Encyclical *Veritatis Splendor* (August 6, 1993), no. 79, http://w2.vatican.va/content/john-paul-ii/en/encyclicals/documents/hf_jp-ii_enc_06081993_veritatis-splendor.html.

A Book of Hours was a devotional tool often used by laypeople. It is an abbreviated form of a breviary, which is a book that contains the prayers and readings of the Divine Office. Although many Books of Hours in common use were simply adorned, many of these books were beautifully illuminated, such as this one from Bruges, Belgium, ca. 1500.

so. The book containing the psalms, prayers, canticles, and readings of the Divine Office is called a breviary.

Benediction

The majesty of the Church and the presence of Christ is felt strongly during the service known as Benediction. During the singing of the hymn "O Salutaris Hostia" ("O Saving Victim"), a priest places a consecrated Host (bread that has been changed into the Body of Christ during the Mass) in a monstrance. A monstrance is usually an ornate vessel with a window through which the Host, or Blessed Sacrament, can be seen. The priest then incenses the Blessed Sacrament. A period of prayer and adoration follows, during which the Divine Praises may be prayed. At the end of the period of adoration, the priest blesses the congregation with the monstrance and then returns the consecrated Host to the tabernacle. There may be a concluding prayer or hymn.

Benediction provides an opportunity for Catholics to adore Jesus in the Blessed Sacrament.

Corpus Christi Procession

In August 1264, Pope Urban IV declared that a feast in honor of Corpus Christi (the Body of Christ) would be held annually on the Thursday after Trinity Sunday. Thursday was chosen for this feast because it was on Holy Thursday that Christ offered His Body and Blood in the Holy Eucharist.

In medieval times, members of Europe's royal families led elaborate processions in which consecrated Eucharistic Hosts were carried through the streets. Bells were rung to tell townspeople that Christ was coming.

In modern times, Corpus Christi processions give Catholics opportunities to display their faith publicly. Parishes organize processions with the permission of the local bishop. Hymns may be sung

Corpus Christi procession

as the faithful walk through their neighborhoods. The procession is usually led by a priest carrying a monstrance containing the Eucharist.

Corpus Christi has become a movable feast. In the United States, it is celebrated on the Sunday after Trinity Sunday. Other countries have continued to celebrate it on a Thursday.

In 2017, Pope Francis moved the Vatican's Corpus Christi observance from a Thursday to a Sunday because he thought that more people would be able to participate on a weekend and because he wanted to align the Vatican's calendar with the liturgical calendar of Italy.

Stations of the Cross

On Fridays during Lent, Catholics traditionally reflect upon the Stations of the Cross, fourteen memorable events that occurred from the moment Christ was condemned to death to His placement in the tomb. During the Crusades (1095–1270), pilgrims visited the Holy Land to walk the path taken by Christ. For Catholics who did not have the opportunity to visit the Holy Land, churches began erecting wooden images of the stations outside, and

THE STATIONS OF THE CROSS

1. Jesus is condemned to death.
2. Jesus bears His Cross.
3. Jesus falls for the first time.
4. Jesus meets His sorrowful Mother.
5. Jesus is helped by Simon.
6. Veronica wipes the face of Jesus.
7. Jesus falls for the second time.
8. Jesus speaks to the women of Jerusalem.
9. Jesus falls for the third time.
10. Jesus is stripped of His garments.
11. Jesus is nailed to the Cross.
12. Jesus dies on the Cross.
13. Jesus is taken down from the Cross.
14. Jesus is laid in the tomb.

During the Crusades, depictions of the Station were erected outdoors for those who could not complete a pilgrimage to the Holy Land to walk the path of Christ. Today, they typically adorn the walls of Catholic churches.

eventually, images of the stations were placed inside churches. The Franciscan priest St. Leonard of Port Maurice promoted the Stations of the Cross in the 1700s and erected hundreds of Stations throughout Italy.

Catholics reflect upon the Stations of the Cross as a way of spiritually walking and praying with Christ as He journeys to the place of His Crucifixion. The stations are usually placed around the inside perimeter of a church. It is customary to genuflect at each station, meditate upon the scene, and say, "We adore You, O Christ, and we bless You; because by Your holy Cross, You have redeemed the world."

Forty Hours Devotion

The number forty has significance in salvation history. When Noah entered his ark, rain fell for forty days and forty nights. The Israelites wandered in the desert for forty years, and Jesus prayed and fasted in the desert for forty days before He began His public ministry. Lent is observed for forty days.

Catholics participate in a devotion known as Forty Hours. These forty hours are spent in continuous adoration of Jesus in the Blessed Sacrament.

The celebration of the Forty Hours devotion begins with a Solemn Mass of Exposition. At the end of the Mass, the Blessed Sacrament is placed on the altar in a monstrance for adoration. The church doors remain unlocked and someone is always present to adore the Lord during the forty hours.

The Blessed Sacrament may be temporarily placed back in the tabernacle while a Mass is said but is returned to its place on the altar until the period of forty hours ends.

The Forty Hours devotion has been part of the Catholic Church since at least the 1200s, although recognition and requirements have varied.[4] On November 25, 1592, Pope Clement VIII formally established the devotion with his papal decree *Graves et diuturnae*. Sts. Philip Neri (1515–1595) and Ignatius of Loyola (1491–1556) promoted the Forty Hours devotion in the 1500s, and St. John Neumann (1811–1860), bishop of Philadelphia, promoted it in the United States in the 1800s. The 1917 *Code of Canon Law* required churches to practice this devotion annually. The 1983 *Code of Canon Law* encouraged but did not require churches to host the Forty Hours devotion.

Veneration of the Cross

The Cross is one of the most recognizable symbols of the Faith. Catholics honor the Cross in a special way by venerating it on Good Friday.

According to legend, circa 326, St. Helena, mother of the emperor Constantine, visited the Holy Land in hopes of finding the Cross on which Jesus was crucified. She oversaw excavations that uncovered three crosses near what was believed to be the crucifixion site. A woman who was gravely ill was brought to the site to be touched by each of the crosses. When the woman touched the third cross, she was instantly cured. That miracle led St. Helena to believe that she had identified the actual Cross that had held the body of Jesus.

St. Helena's discovery of the True Cross is celebrated every year on May 7 in the Chapel of the Finding of the True Cross, in the Church of the Holy Sepulchre in Jerusalem. On that date, a piece of wood from the True Cross is carried in

Legend holds that St. Helena, mother of the emperor Constantine, oversaw excavations that uncovered the True Cross of Christ.

procession to the place where tradition says it was found. In the seventh century, the Church in Rome adopted this practice of venerating a fragment of the True Cross on Good Friday.

Today, a large wooden cross or crucifix, rather than a fragment of the True Cross, is used for the Veneration of the Cross during the celebration of the Lord's Passion on Good Friday. The cross is placed near the sanctuary, and one by one, clergy and laypeople approach the cross and genuflect, kiss the cross, or offer another sign of respect.

4   D.D. Emmons, "Forty Hours Devotion," *Our Sunday Visitor Newsweekly*, April 6, 2010, https://www.osv.com/OSVNews-weekly/Article/TabId/535/ArtMID/13567/ArticleID/3512/Forty-Hours-Devotion.aspx.

Venerating Relics

A relic is defined as "the body, or part of a body, of a saint, or anything, such as clothing, associated with the saint which the Church venerates because of the sanctity of the person while on earth."[5] There are three classes of relics. First-class relics include physical remains of a saint, such as hair, bones, or the incorrupt body. Second-class relics are items that were used by a saint on a regular basis, including the saint's clothing or a book that he carried constantly.

Most relics owned by laypersons are third-class relics, items that have touched a first- or second-class relic. For example, some Catholics wear medals that contain a relic of a favorite saint. That relic is usually a small piece of cloth that was touched to a first- or second-class relic of that saint.

Relics are only objects, so Catholics do not pray to them. Catholics ask the saints associated with the relics to intercede for them in heaven.

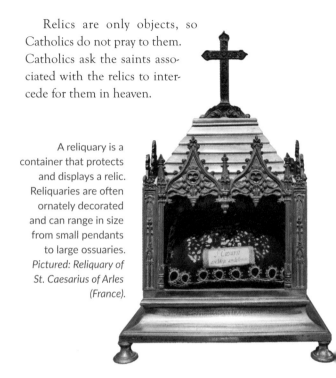

A reliquary is a container that protects and displays a relic. Reliquaries are often ornately decorated and can range in size from small pendants to large ossuaries. *Pictured: Reliquary of St. Caesarius of Arles (France).*

---

5   Father Bennet Kelley, C.P., *The New St. Joseph Baltimore Catechism*, official rev. ed., no. 2 (New York: Catholic Book Publishing, 1969), 249.

CHAPTER 5

PRIVATE CATHOLIC DEVOTIONS

In addition to attending Mass, Catholics strengthen their relationship with God through private devotions. Although praying with others can lead to joyful fellowship, it is important to set aside time for quiet private prayer.

Prayers

The Catholic Church has suggested many ways to engage in private prayer and follow St. Paul's call to "pray constantly" (1 Thess. 5:17).

The Angelus and the Regina Caeli

In many places, including Vatican City, bells are rung at 6:00 a.m., noon, and 6:00 p.m. to call the faithful to pray the Angelus. The call of the Angelus bell unites Catholics in prayer.

The practice of praying the Angelus three times each day is believed to have started with Italian monks in the eleventh century who ended their day by saying three Hail Marys. In subsequent years, many Church leaders encouraged their congregations to begin and end the day by saying three Hail Marys. Prayers began to be said at noon in remembrance of Christ's Crucifixion at midday.

The Angelus recalls the Annunciation and Mary's fiat:

> V. The Angel of the Lord declared to Mary:
> R. And she conceived of the Holy Spirit.
> *Hail Mary, full of grace, the Lord is with thee; blessed art thou among women and blessed is the fruit of thy womb, Jesus. Holy Mary, Mother of God, pray for us sinners, now and at the hour of our death. Amen.*
> V. Behold the handmaid of the Lord:
> R. Be it done unto me according to Thy word.
> *Hail Mary ...*
> V. And the Word was made Flesh:
> R. And dwelt among us.
> *Hail Mary ...*
> V. Pray for us, O Holy Mother of God,

The Holy Father leads the faithful in praying the Angelus at noon on Sundays and holy days from the window of his study overlooking St. Peter's Square.

> R. That we may be made worthy of the promises of Christ.
> Let us pray: Pour forth, we beseech You, O Lord, Your grace into our hearts; that we, to whom the Incarnation of Christ, Your Son, was made known by the message of an angel, may by His Passion and Cross be brought to the glory of His Resurrection, through the same Christ our Lord. Amen.

The Regina Caeli is an ancient Latin hymn, one of four seasonal Marian antiphons, traditionally sung from the Easter Vigil through Pentecost.

During the Easter season, the Regina Caeli is prayed in place of the Angelus.

> V. Queen of Heaven, rejoice, alleluia.
> R. For He whom you did merit to bear, alleluia.
> V. Has risen, as He said, alleluia.
> R. Pray for us to God, alleluia.
> V. Rejoice and be glad, O Virgin Mary, alleluia.
> R. For the Lord has truly risen, alleluia.
> Let us pray: O God, who gave joy to the world through the resurrection of Your Son, our Lord Jesus Christ, grant we beseech You, that through the intercession of the Virgin Mary, His Mother, we may obtain the joys of everlasting life. Through the same Christ our Lord. Amen.

Daily Mass

Catholics must attend Mass each Sunday (or the preceding Saturday evening), but they are encouraged to go beyond this obligation and attend Mass every day. Every time they go to Mass, Catholics have an opportunity to receive Holy Communion and grace.

To emphasize the importance of daily Mass, Pope Francis initiated a practice of saying an early-morning Mass for all Vatican employees whenever he is in Rome.[1] Many churches in the United States offer daily morning or evening Masses so laypersons can attend before or after work.

Grace before Meals

Grace is a short prayer of thanksgiving. The importance of mealtime prayer is seen in Deuteronomy

---

[1]   Cindy Wooden, "Pope's Daily Mass Shows Sharing Liturgy Is Form of Service, Bishop Says," Catholic News Service, April 24, 2013, http://www.catholicnews.com/services/englishnews/2013/pope-s-daily-mass-shows-sharing-liturgy-is-form-of-service-bishop-says.cfm.

8:10, where Moses says, "And you shall eat and be full, and you shall bless the LORD your God for the good land he has given you." Acts 27:35 tells us that St. Paul "took bread, and giving thanks to God in the presence of all … broke it and began to eat."

In Catholic homes and schools, children learn to say grace before meals. This is usually a simple prayer that can be learned quickly, such as this traditional version:

> Bless us, O Lord, and these Thy gifts which we are about to receive from Thy bounty, through Christ our Lord. Amen.

Members of the clergy often observe much more formal practices for offering grace before meals. The *Rule of St. Benedict*, a guide to monastic living that many religious orders follow, includes a section with details on praying and blessing food before meals.

Guardian Angel Prayer

> Angel of God, my guardian dear
> To whom God's love commits me here
> Ever this day, be at my side
> To light and guard, to rule and guide.
> Amen.

One of the first prayers that Catholic children learn is directed to their guardian angels.

The Guardian Angel Prayer has been part of Catholic life since at least the 1100s. It was included in the writings of St. Anselm (ca. 1103–1109), but he is not believed to be the author. A version was published in the *Baltimore Manual of Prayers* in 1888.

The *Catechism of the Catholic Church* explains that each individual has a guardian angel (no. 336); this was emphasized by Pope Benedict XVI in 2011 when he wrote, "Dear friends, the Lord is ever close and active in humanity's history and accompanies us with the unique presence of his Angels, whom today the Church venerates as 'Guardian Angels', that is, *ministers of the divine care for every human being*. From the beginning until the hour of death, human life is surrounded by their constant protection."[2]

The feast of the Guardian Angels is celebrated on October 2.

Litanies

A litany is a public or private prayer of praise or petition. When said by a group, a leader reads an invocation or a petition, and other participants give a response. The Litany of the Blessed Virgin Mary, Mother of Life, for example, is a prayer of petition to ask Mary to protect unborn children. After each phrase said by a leader, followers respond, "Mary, pray for us." Individuals can also offer this litany privately by saying both parts.

Well-known litanies include those of the Sacred Heart of Jesus, of the Most Precious Blood, and of the Holy Name of Jesus.

Novenas

When Catholics wish to pray for a special intention, they often pray a novena. A novena (from the Latin word for nine) is usually a prayer of petition that is said on nine consecutive days, but sometimes it is prayed during nine consecutive months. It is prayed for nine days or months in remembrance of the nine days during which the apostles prayed together after Jesus ascended into heaven. Some of the best-known novenas are the Miraculous Medal Novena, the Divine Mercy Novena, and the Novena to the Sacred Heart.

Mother Teresa, now known as St. Teresa of Calcutta, jokingly stated that she couldn't wait

---

[2]   Benedict XVI, Angelus address, October 2, 2011.

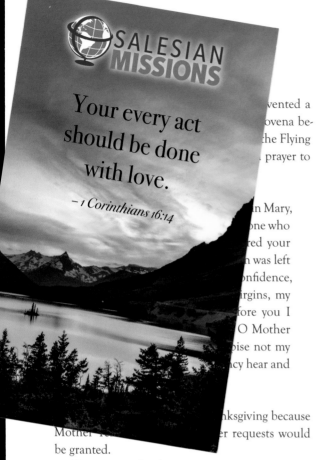

Your every act
should be done
with love.

– 1 Corinthians 16:14

vented a
ovena be-
the Flying
prayer to

n Mary,
ne who
ed your
was left
nfidence,
rgins, my
ore you I
O Mother
ise not my
cy hear and

ksgiving because
requests would
be granted.

Her spiritual adviser, Msgr. Leo Maasburg, stated, "Mother Teresa used this prayer constantly: for petitions for the cure of a sick child, before important discussions or when passports went missing, to request heavenly aid when the fuel supply was running short on a night-time mission and the destination was still far away in the darkness."[3]

Prayers for the Dead

Catholics believe that after their death, some souls go to purgatory, a place of purification for those who died in the mercy of God but are still not perfectly purified. Catholics pray for the dead because the souls in purgatory need prayers to help relieve them of their sufferings and help them journey to heaven.

Acts of Consecration

When a Catholic makes an act of consecration, he expresses his desire to move away from bad influences and work toward a closer relationship with God. Usually the Catholic consecrates his life to Christ, to Mary, or to a saint to guide him as he tries to obey and serve God. The act of consecration can be made publicly with a service in a church, or it can be a private declaration to follow a holier path in life.

Acts of Reparation

Through an act of reparation, a Catholic prays to make amends for wrongs he or others have done. An act of reparation may be said privately to show remorse for unacceptable behavior or it may be said in a group setting to offer an apology for everyone's sins.

[3] Quoted in Joseph Pronechen, "How to Pray Mother Teresa's Famous 'Flying Novena' to Our Lady," *National Catholic Register*, August 30, 2016, http://www.ncregister.com/blog/joseph-pronechen/mother-teresas-express-line-to-heaven-novena.

Practices

Whereas prayers can often be said anytime and anywhere, some Catholic devotions are associated with certain times and places.

Eucharistic Adoration

Eucharistic Adoration is the practice of adoring the Blessed Sacrament exposed in a monstrance. Although Christ is honored in the Blessed Sacrament during Mass, it is important for Catholics to spend some quiet time in Eucharistic Adoration outside of Mass. It is a time to read Scripture or pray privately in the presence of Christ in the Eucharist.

From his ordination to the final days of his papacy, Pope St. John Paul II delivered homilies and wrote encyclicals stressing the benefits of Eucharistic Adoration. He encouraged parishes to establish times in which the faithful could come to church just to adore the

A monstrance is used to expose the Blessed Sacrament during Eucharistic Adoration. It can also be used for Benediction, Forty Hours devotion, and Corpus Christi processions.

Eucharist. "The Church and the world have great need of Eucharistic Adoration," he wrote. "Jesus waits for us in this sacrament of love. Let us be generous with our time in going to meet Him in adoration and contemplation full of faith."[4]

St. Teresa of Calcutta agreed. She stated, "Perpetual Eucharistic Adoration with exposition needs a great push. People ask me: 'What will convert America and save the world?' My answer is prayer. What we need is for every parish to come before Jesus in the Blessed Sacrament in holy hours of prayer."[5]

Divine Mercy Devotions

From 1928 to 1938, Christ appeared to St. Faustina Kowalska and urged her to spread devotion to His Divine Mercy. He taught her the Chaplet of Divine Mercy and encouraged her to pray it especially for sinners and for the sick and the dying. Although prayers are appropriate at any time of the day, it is suggested that the Divine Mercy Chaplet be said at 3:00 p.m. or during the 3:00 hour in memory of the hour in which Christ died on the Cross.

Christ asked that the chaplet be recited as a novena and gave St. Faustina specific intentions for each of the nine days. The novena is usually prayed beginning on Good Friday, leading up to Divine Mercy Sunday, the Sunday after Easter. On April

---

[4] John Paul II, Letter *Dominicae Cenae* (February 24, 1980), no. 3.

[5] "The Spirituality of Blessed Mother Teresa of Calcutta—in Her Own Words," Missionaries of the Blessed Sacrament, http://www.acfp2000.com/Saints/Mother_Teresa/Mother_Teresa.html.

30, 2000, the day he canonized St. Faustina, Pope St. John Paul II established this feast for the universal Church.

Christ promised St. Faustina that those devoted to His Divine Mercy would receive great mercy at the hour of death. He said, "I desire that the Feast of Mercy be a refuge and shelter for all souls, and especially for poor sinners. On that day the very depths of My tender mercy are open. I pour out a whole ocean of graces upon those souls who approach the fount of My mercy. The soul that will go to Confession and receive Holy Communion shall obtain complete forgiveness of sins and punishment."[6]

Fasting

In the Catholic Church, fasting refers to refraining from eating or drinking during a set period as an act of penance. Fasting is required of Catholics on Ash Wednesday and Good Friday. According to the United States Conference of Catholic Bishops: "The norms on fasting are obligatory from age eighteen until age fifty-nine. When fasting, a person is permitted to eat one full meal, as well as two smaller meals that together are not equal to a full meal." Fasting should not, however, interfere with one's health. Individuals with medical conditions that require regularly scheduled meals and medication are exempt from fasting requirements, as are the sick and pregnant or nursing mothers.

---

[6] St. Maria Faustina Kowalska, *Divine Mercy in My Soul* (Stockbridge, MA: Congregation of Marians of the Immaculate Conception, 1987), no. 699.

PRAYING THE DIVINE MERCY CHAPLET

Christ promised St. Faustina that those devoted to His Divine Mercy would receive great mercy at the hour of death. To pray the Divine Mercy Chaplet, use any five decade rosary. Begin by making the Sign of the Cross, then:

1. Pray one Our Father, one Hail Mary, and the Apostles' Creed.

2. Then, on the Our Father bead that starts each decade say the following prayer:

   Eternal Father, I offer You the Body and Blood, Soul and Divinity of Your dearly beloved Son, our Lord Jesus Christ, in atonement for our sins and those of the whole world.

3. On the ten beads of each decade, pray:

   For the sake of His sorrowful Passion, have mercy on us and on the whole world.

4. After praying each of the five decades, conclude by reciting the following prayer three times:

   Holy God, Holy Mighty One, Holy Immortal One, have mercy on us and on the whole world.

You may also wish to pray additional optional prayers that begin and end the Chaplet. These can be found online at **thedivinemercy.org**.

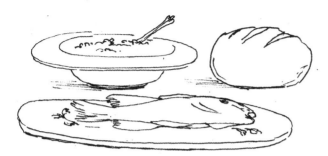

Fridays during Lent are days of abstinence from meat, so fish makes a good choice for meals. Many Catholics practice Friday abstinence throughout the year.

Friday Abstinence

In honor of the day on which Christ died for us, Friday has long been considered a day of penance. One form this penance took was the traditional abstinence from eating meat on Fridays—which many Catholics still observe. In their 1966 *Pastoral Statement on Penance and Abstinence*, the United States Conference of Catholic Bishops lessened the requirement to abstaining from meat only on Fridays during Lent, for healthy Catholics between the ages of fourteen and fifty-nine. The statement reminds Catholics, however, that every Friday is still a penitential day and encourages the faithful to make "every Friday a day of self-denial and mortification in prayerful remembrance of the passion of Jesus Christ" (no. 23).

Indulgences

Catholics make a confession and receive the sacrament of Penance to ask forgiveness for sins. They might also seek indulgences.

The *Code of Canon Law* (can. 992) and the *Catechism of the Catholic Church* (no. 1471) state:

> An indulgence is a remission before God of the temporal punishment due to sins whose guilt has already been forgiven, which the faithful Christian who is duly disposed gains under certain prescribed conditions through the action of the Church which, as the minister of redemption, dispenses and applies with authority the treasury of the satisfactions of Christ and the saints.

This definition uses the terms "temporal punishment" and "sins whose guilt has already been forgiven." Temporal punishment is that which will end. For example, parents might punish a disobedient child by saying that he cannot watch television for one hour. When that hour has passed, the punishment ends. Some sins might deserve temporal punishment that can be served on earth by prayer and charitable works or can be served in purgatory.

Why is temporal punishment given for sins that have already been forgiven? A sin might be forgiven, but there could still be a debt to pay. Your neighbor might forgive you if you were playing ball and accidentally broke his window. Although you have been forgiven, you should still pay your debt by replacing the window.

There are two types of indulgences, *plenary* (full) and *partial*. One might receive a partial indulgence if only a portion of the conditions for the indulgence were met.

There are many specific indulgences, such as the Divine Mercy and the All Souls' Day indulgences. Although each has specific conditions, an individual usually must receive the sacraments of Penance and Holy Eucharist and pray for the intentions of the pope within a specific time period in order to receive an indulgence.

Prior to 1968, many Catholic prayer books and holy cards listed ways in which one could earn an indulgence for a specified number of days or years. Some mistakenly thought that meant that someone who earned, for example, a thirty-day indulgence could move from purgatory to heaven a month sooner. Pope Paul VI ended this confusion when he oversaw the revision of the *Enchiridion Indulgentiarum* (Collection of Indulgences). He explained that because heaven and purgatory do not operate on the earthly calendar, the notion of days and nights does not have the same meaning after death. Instead of equating indulgences with a specific number of days or years, indulgences should be considered in terms of a certain amount of penance or reparation for sins.[7]

Penance

The word *penance* has two meanings for Catholics. Penance can be another name for the sacrament of Reconciliation, the sacrament in which sins are confessed, or it can refer to prayers and sacrifices made to atone for wrongdoing. And the two meanings are related.

After a priest hears someone's confession in the sacrament of Reconciliation, he assigns him a penance. The penance consists of one or more prayers or acts the individual must do in order for his sins to be forgiven. For example, a priest might say, "For your penance say three Hail Marys" or "Write a note of apology to your teacher." As the *Catechism* explains:

> Many sins wrong our neighbor. One must do what is possible in order to repair the harm (e.g., return stolen goods, restore the reputation of someone slandered, pay compensation for injuries). Simple justice requires as much. But sin also injures and weakens the sinner himself, as well as his relationships with God and neighbor. Absolution [the remission of sin] takes away sin, but it does not remedy all

the disorders sin has caused.[8] Raised up from sin, the sinner must still recover his full spiritual health by doing something more to make amends for the sin: he must "make satisfaction for" or "expiate" his sins. This satisfaction is also called "penance." (no. 1459)

Sacred Heart/First Friday Devotions

First Friday Masses are dedicated to the Sacred Heart of Jesus. In the 1600s, Christ appeared to a young nun now known as St. Margaret Mary Alacoque and asked her to encourage the faithful to receive Holy Communion on the first Friday of nine consecutive months with the intention of making reparation to His Sacred Heart for people's sins and ingratitude and to offer each Holy Communion as an act of atonement for offenses against the Blessed Sacrament. Christ promised that those who followed this practice would receive mercy when they died.

The nun reported the visions of Christ to her superiors, who dismissed them as delusions. After years of ridicule, she finally gained respect in 1686 when a newly elected superior, Mother Melin, said that the nuns could observe a private feast day for the Sacred Heart within the walls of the convent.

On May 8, 1873, Pope Pius IX granted approval for Catholics to participate in devotion to the Sacred Heart.

First Saturday Devotions

During one of her apparitions to Lucia dos Santos (1907–2005), Our Lady of Fatima gave her specific instructions to set aside the first Saturday of five

---

[7] Paul VI, *Indulgentiarum Doctrina* (An Apostolic Constitution on Indulgences) (January 1, 1967), https://www.ewtn.com/library/PAPALDOC/P6INDULG.HTM.

[8] Cf. Council of Trent (1551): DS 1712.

consecutive months for prayers in honor of and in reparation for sins against the Immaculate Heart of Mary. On those first Saturdays, the Blessed Mother asked the faithful to attend Mass, receive Holy Communion, pray the Rosary, and spend fifteen minutes meditating on the mysteries of the Rosary. The faithful should also go to confession within eight days of the first Saturday. Catholics continue the practice of First Saturday Devotions in honor of the Immaculate Heart of Mary.

The Sacred Heart of Jesus

ENTHRONEMENT OF THE SACRED HEART

The tradition of dedicating a home to the Sacred Heart comes from the writing of St. Margaret Mary Alacoque: "That all those who are devoted to this Sacred Heart will never perish and that, since He is the source of all blessings, He will shower them in abundance on every place where an image of this loving heart shall be exposed to be loved and honored."[1]

It is believed that in 1675, Jesus appeared to St. Margaret Mary and promised her, "I will establish peace in their homes. I will bless every place where a picture of My Heart shall be exposed and honored."[2] In remembrance of this promise, Catholics may engage in a Home Enthronement ceremony, in which they dedicate their homes to the Sacred Heart and place a Sacred Heart picture or statue in a place of honor. This practice has been endorsed by four popes: Pius X, Benedict XV, Pius XI, and Pius XII. Families who enthrone the Sacred Heart in their homes recognize and acknowledge Jesus' loving kingship over them.

---

[1] "Enthronement of the Sacred Heart of Jesus in the Home," EWTN, https://olrl.org/pray/enthrone.shtml.

[2] "The Promises of Our Lord to Saint Margaret Mary for Souls Devoted to His Sacred Heart," EWTN, https://www.ewtn.com/faith/teachings/incab2.htm.

Marian Devotions

"To Jesus through Mary" is a popular phrase heard in Catholic homes, schools, and churches. Catholics show devotion to Mary and ask her to bring their prayers to her Son, Jesus Christ.

The Hail Mary

At the beginning of the twelfth century, religious leaders, particularly those guiding monastic orders, began to gather Mary legends, anecdotes of appearances and devotions to Mary. Referring to the Gospel of St. Luke, they used the angel Gabriel's and Elizabeth's greetings to Mary as a devotion and recited the words, "Hail Mary, full of grace, the Lord is with thee. Blessed art thou among women, and blessed is the fruit of thy womb, Jesus."

By 1184, the Archbishop of Canterbury was encouraging everyone to use the Hail Mary greeting as a prayer. In 1196, the Bishop of Paris, Eudes de Sully, issued a synodal decree urging priests to make certain that all who attended their churches knew the Hail Mary as well as the Lord's Prayer and the Apostles' Creed. The Synod of Durham

issued a similar decree for the people of England in 1217.

Despite support from Church leaders, there were criticisms that the Hail Mary was merely a greeting rather than a prayer because it did not contain a bid or request. The petition "Holy Mary, Mother of God, pray for us sinners" was added to settle this dispute. Although the exact date of the revision is unknown, there are examples that date to the 1400s. The full version is included in the French edition of the *Calendar of Shepherds*, published in 1493, and the British museum owns a work by Savonarola created in 1495 that includes the full Hail Mary prayer.

The Hail Mary known in the twenty-first century includes the longer petition "Holy Mary, Mother of God, pray for us sinners now and at the hour of our death."

The Rosary

The Rosary, a series of prayers that many Catholics pray, is said to have been developed by St. Dominic in 1208 after he saw a vision of Mary.

"Rosary" is also the name of the circular string of beads used to pray this prayer. The beads are in groups of ten, known as decades, separated by single beads, and with a separate string of five beads and a crucifix extending from the circle. The Hail Mary is said on the small beads, and the Our Father is said on the single beads between each decade. Although the series of prayers may seem repetitive, the United States Conference of Catholic Bishops reminds us that "the gentle repetition of the words helps us to enter into the silence of our hearts, where Christ's spirit dwells."[9]

While praying the Rosary, one reflects upon the mysteries of the Rosary which are significant events in the life of Christ and His Mother, Mary. There are four sets of mysteries: the Joyful Mysteries, usually prayed on Mondays and Saturdays; the Sorrowful Mysteries, usually prayed on Tuesdays and Fridays; the Glorious Mysteries, usually prayed on Wednesdays and Sundays; and the Luminous Mysteries, usually prayed on Thursdays. (For a list of all the mysteries, see page 50). The seasonal exceptions are that the Joyful Mysteries are remembered on Sundays during the Christmas Season and the Sorrowful Mysteries on Sundays during Lent.

How to Pray the Rosary

1. Make the Sign of the Cross, hold the crucifix, and say the Apostles' Creed.
2. Say the Our Father on the first bead that follows the Crucifix.
3. Say a Hail Mary on each of the three beads that follow, asking God for an increase in the theological virtues of faith, hope, and love.
4. Say the Glory Be on the chain between the last Hail Mary bead and the next bead.

The main panel on this miniature altarpiece, *The Fifteen Mysteries and the Virgin of the Rosary*, features the Virgin Mary holding Christ, who has woven a garland of roses from each prayer of the Rosary recited.

---

[9] United States Conference of Catholic Bishops, "How to Pray the Rosary," http://www.usccb.org/prayer-and-worship/prayers-and-devotions/rosaries/how-to-pray-the-rosary.cfm.

5. Reflect upon the first mystery and then say the Our Father on the next bead.

6. Say a Hail Mary on each of the ten beads that follow.

7. Say the Glory Be on the chain that follows the decade.

8. After the Glory Be, an optional prayer known as the Fatima Decade Prayer is often added: O my Jesus, forgive us our sins, save us from the fires of hell, lead all souls to heaven, especially those most in need of Thy mercy.[10]

9. Reflect upon the second mystery and then say one Our Father on the large bead.

10. Repeat these steps as you continue through the third, fourth and fifth decades.

11. Say the prayer of Hail Holy Queen.

12. Make the Sign of the Cross.

Styles of Rosary

There are many forms of the rosary but the most widely known is the Dominican rosary, which consists of five groups of ten beads (Hail Mary beads). Each group of ten beads is known as a decade. A larger bead, known as the Our Father bead, is placed between each decade. A medal sits at the center of the rosary. A cross or crucifix is placed at the beginning.

The World Mission Rosary

In the 1950s, Archbishop Fulton J. Sheen was the voice of Catholicism on radio and television. His broadcast career began in 1950 with the weekly radio program *The Catholic Hour*. By 1956, he had

added a television program, *Life Is Worth Living*, which reached thirty million people each week. In addition to his broadcast duties, Archbishop Sheen served as the national director for the Society of the Propagation of the Faith from 1950 to 1966. In service to the missions, he developed the World Mission Rosary.

Each decade of the World Mission Rosary has beads of a different color, and each color represents a continent. Blue represents Australia and the oceans of the Pacific. Green honors Africa and its rich grasslands. White has been chosen as the color for Europe because that is the site of the Vatican. Asia is represented by yellow, the color of the rising sun. Red symbolizes the Americas and the spiritual fire of immigrants whose faith brought them to new lands.

During a February 1951 radio broadcast, Archbishop Sheen introduced the World Mission Rosary and invited listeners to order it and pray for everyone in the world, especially the poor and the vulnerable. He said, "When the Rosary is completed, one has ... embraced all continents, all people, in prayer.... Won't you please make a tour of the world on your World Mission Rosary?"[11]

---

[10] When Mary appeared to three children in Fatima on July 13, 1917, she asked them to say this prayer after each mystery of the Rosary.

[11] "World Mission Rosary," Society for the Propagation of the Faith, Mission Office of the Archdiocese of Chicago, December 18, 2014, http://www.wearemissionary.org/world-mission-rosary-2/.

THE MYSTERIES OF THE ROSARY

The Joyful Mysteries
Usually prayed on Monday and Saturday

The Annunciation of the Lord to Mary
The Visitation of Mary to Elizabeth
The Nativity of Our Lord and Savior Jesus Christ
The Presentation of Our Lord in the Temple
The Finding of the Child Jesus in the Temple by Mary and Joseph

The Sorrowful Mysteries
Usually prayed on Tuesday and Friday

The Agony of Jesus in the Garden
The Scourging of Jesus at the Pillar
The Crowning of Jesus with Thorns
The Carrying of the Cross
The Crucifixion of Our Lord

The Glorious Mysteries
Usually prayed on Wednesday and Sunday

The Resurrection of Our Lord
The Ascension of Our Lord into Heaven
The Descent of the Holy Spirit at Pentecost
The Assumption of the Blessed Virgin Mary into Heaven
The Coronation of the Virgin Mary

The Luminous Mysteries
Usually prayed on Thursday

The Baptism of Christ in the Jordan River
The Wedding at Cana
The Proclamation of the Kingdom of God
The Transfiguration
The Institution of the Eucharist at the Last Supper

The World Mission Rosary was sold to raise funds for missionary work and to encourage prayer for those suffering on all continents.

Military Rosaries

Throughout history, military personnel have carried religious articles with them on the battlefield. During World War I, chaplains of the United States Armed Services distributed metal rosaries called pull-chain rosaries because the links resembled those seen on lamp chains. First made in 1916, these metal rosaries were thought to be strong enough to survive rough treatment on the battlefield.

Collectors will find that authentic military rosaries that were carried into battle will be dulled or blued rather than shiny silver. Military personnel deliberately darkened their silver rosaries so that they would not shine and reveal a soldier's location to the enemy.

Irish Rosaries

The Rosary has played such a large role in the lives of the Irish that it has been called the Irish catechism. Irish rosaries are made with natural materials found in the country, such as bogwood and marble as well as man-made materials, including crystal. Many Irishmen have made their living by making rosaries in factories or by obtaining the raw materials to produce them.

The opening of the Mitchell Rosary Factory in 1927 was a joyous occasion for the people of Dublin. Young girls found jobs in the factory. Married women with children picked up beads at the factory, strung them at home, and were paid for their labor. These beads, however, were made of animal horn. Factory workers boiled the horn in large vats to soften it for bead making.

The large vats of boiling horn produced extremely strong, unpleasant odors that bothered the people of Dublin. Due to the many objections of Dublin residents, the Mitchell Rosary Factory was forced to stop making horn rosaries around 1960.

Knotted-Cord Rosaries

Historians have traced the introduction of the knotted-cord rosary to around 800 to 900 in Ireland and other European countries, where monks made knots in long cords and then fingered those knots as they said their prayers. Most knotted-cord rosaries are made entirely of twine with a woven cross at the top of the pendant. Others have a plastic or metal cross or crucifix at the top.

Knotted-cord rosaries are handmade and have become a project of many religious organizations and school groups. The Rosary Army, for example, distributes free corded rosaries and instructions for making them. Their motto is, "Make them. Pray them. Give them away."[12]

A knotted-cord rosary

[12] See the website of the Rosary Army, http://rosaryarmy.newevangelizers.com/.

Praying to Saints

There is a common misconception that Catholics pray to saints as they pray to God. The truth is that Catholics do not pray to saints but rather they ask the saints to pray with them and for them.

Special Patron Saints

The Church uses the word *patrons* when referring to saints who are special guardians or intercessors for particular persons, places, causes, or occupations. St. Joan of Arc is the patron of soldiers because she did God's work by traveling with an army. St. Charles Borromeo is the patron of catechists and seminarians because he founded seminaries and devoted himself to providing education for the clergy. Among the many institutions named for this saint is St. Charles Borromeo Seminary in Philadelphia, Pennsylvania, noted for educating priests, deacons, and laypeople to serve the Catholic Church. Patron saints provide inspiration to achieve goals and follow Christ's teaching.

Have you ever asked a friend to pray for you? Just as we rely on our friends to pray for us, we ask the saints in heaven to join with us in prayer and take our prayers to God. For particular intentions, we might ask particular saints—the patrons of those intentions—to assist us. For instance, those who are seeking employment might pray to St. Joseph, patron of workers. Not only are the prayers of the saints powerful—"The prayer of a

righteous man has great power" (James 5:16)—but certain saints who have shared our experiences and difficulties have sympathy with us and are especially ready to intercede for us.

St. Joseph

St. Joseph, the husband of Mary and foster father of Jesus, always found safe shelter for his family. When there was no room at the inn on Christmas Eve, he brought his wife, Mary, to a warm stable. He sheltered his family in Egypt when King Herod threatened the life of his Son, Jesus. Because he provided for his family, St. Joseph is known as the patron saint of the home. He has two feast days: March 19, the Solemnity of St. Joseph, the Spouse of the Blessed Virgin Mary, and May 1, the feast of St. Joseph the Worker.

St. Nicholas

St. Nicholas (270-343) was the bishop of Myra, in Lycia. When he was very young, his parents died and left him a large inheritance, which he shared with children and adults in need. Legends say that when Nicholas learned of three sisters who had no money for

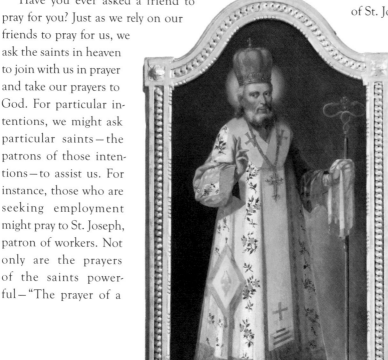

St. Nicholas,
Bishop of Myra

a dowry, he threw three bags of gold through their window one night so that they could marry. Consequently, St. Nicholas has become the patron saint of brides as well as the patron saint of children.

St. Nicholas, and especially the legend of his generosity toward the three sisters, is the inspiration for Santa Claus (Sinterklaas in Dutch). Many Christmas season traditions and foods have roots in his story. His feast day is December 6.

St. Michael, the Archangel

St. Michael, although an archangel and not a saint, is considered the patron saint of police officers, soldiers, and firefighters. He is the leader of God's army of angels and combats Satan and evil in the world (see Rev. 12:7). The name Michael means "Who is like God?" The Church commemorates St. Michael, along with archangels Raphael and Gabriel, on September 29.

St. Patrick

Although Patrick (385–461) was born in England, the Irish have claimed him as their patron because he preached the gospel throughout Ireland. As a child, he was kidnapped by pirates and brought to Ireland, where he was sold as a slave. He spent long hours in prayer while shepherding his master's flock. He later escaped by ship but returned to Ireland after being ordained and spread the Faith there. St. Patrick has a second job as the patron saint of engineers because he encouraged the construction of Irish clay churches and he taught the Irish to build arches of lime mortar rather than dry masonry.[13] His feast day is March 17.

---

[13] "St. Patrick, the Patron Saint of Engineers," *Engineer's Journal*, March 16, 2017, http://www.engineersjournal. ie/2017/03/16/st-patrick-patron-saint-engineers/.

ST. MICHAEL PRAYER

Around the year 1885, Pope Leo XIII was given a vision of demons gathering on Rome. This vision prompted him to compose the Prayer to St. Michael, and he asked it be prayed at the end of each Mass. The practice remained part of the liturgy until 1968 when the new liturgy was authorized. But in 1994 Pope John Paul II urged the faithful to take up the prayer once again in order to battle "against the forces of darkness and against the spirit of this world."

Prayer to St. Michael

St. Michael the Archangel, defend us in battle. Be our defense against the wickedness and snares of the devil. May God rebuke him, we humbly pray, and do thou, O prince of the heavenly hosts, by the power of God, thrust into hell Satan, and all the evil spirits, who prowl about the world seeking the ruin of souls. Amen.

ST. JOSEPH THE REALTOR

Stories abound of Catholics praying to St. Joseph when they wish to sell a house. Although this may seem like a custom started by realtors, the practice has been led by the saints. St. Teresa of Avila was said to have encouraged nuns in her order to pray and bury medals of St. Joseph when they needed land to expand their convent. St. André Bessette, Canada's first native-born male saint, has been credited with bringing the practice to North America.

André Bessette entered the Congregation of the Holy Cross in Montreal in the late 1800s. He kept a small statue of St. Joseph near a window overlooking Mount Royal. Officials of the Holy Cross Congregation had been trying to buy land on Mount Royal for many years, but the owners would not sell. One day, Brother André encouraged a few of his peers to climb Mount Royal with him and plant medals of St. Joseph in the ground. A short time later, the landowners relented and agreed to sell a parcel of land. Then in 1931, the Holy Cross Congregation wished to expand their church, but they lacked the funds. They prayed and buried a statue of St. Joseph in the middle of the potential construction site and soon found the money they needed. The site became known as Saint Joseph's Oratory and is considered to be the world's largest shrine devoted to St. Joseph.

St. Jude

As one of the twelve apostles, St. Jude (first century) had special ties to Jesus. According to legend, King Abagar asked Jude to bring him a picture of Jesus so that he might be cured of leprosy. Jude took the message to Jesus, who responded by pressing the image of His face into a cloth, which Jude took to King Abagar. The king was cured, and Jude became known as one who could intercede for healings. Statues and holy cards of St. Jude often depict him holding an image of Jesus. St. Jude is the patron saint of impossible causes. His feast day is October 28.

St. Lucy

Lucy (ca. 283–303) was born in Syracuse, in Sicily. Although she lived during a time when belief in Christ was punishable by death, St. Lucy clung to her Faith. She was denounced to the governor of Sicily by a young man whom she refused to marry. When she would not renounce her Faith, her enemies had her blinded and then had her killed. St. Lucy has become the patron saint for those who are blind or visually impaired. Her name means "light." Her feast day is December 13.

St. Kateri Tekakwitha

Canonized by Pope Benedict XVI in 2012, Kateri Tekakwitha (1656–1680), known as the Lily of the Mohawks, was the first Native American to become a saint. She was born in upstate New York to an Algonquin mother and a Mohawk father. At age nineteen, Kateri heard the Christian message that Jesuit missionaries brought to her village and was later baptized. Her family rejected her for following the Catholic

Faith and for refusing to marry a Mohawk warrior. Because she had to flee her village, St. Kateri Tekakwitha has become known as the patron saint of those in exile as well as the patron of ecology because she often prayed in the forest. Her feast day is July 14.

St. Thomas More

Lawyers, civil servants, and politicians look to St. Thomas More (1478–1535) as an example of integrity. He was chancellor of England under King Henry VIII but refused to accept the king, rather than the pope, as the head of the Church. Because he would not deny his Faith to remain in the king's good graces, St. Thomas More was martyred. He shares a feast day with Bishop John Fisher, who was also martyred under Henry VIII, on June 22.

St. Benedict

Born into a wealthy family, St. Benedict (480–547) received a rigorous education but later lived in isolation to pray. When he was urged to join and lead a religious community, he developed a guide to monastic life, called the Rule of St. Benedict, that formed the basis for many orders. He is the patron saint of students and of Europe. His feast day is July 11.

St. Thérèse of Lisieux

Thérèse Martin (1873–1897) was born in Alençon, France, and, at the age of fifteen, with special permission, entered the Carmelite monastery in Lisieux. Many have read her autobiography, *The Story of a Soul*. Thérèse is best known for her Little Way: doing many small acts of virtue with great love—a way to grow in holiness that every person can practice. Before she died of tuberculosis at the age of twenty-four, Thérèse promised to spend her heaven doing good on earth. Known as the Little Flower and having loved and written about flowers, Thérèse is the patron saint of florists. She is also a patron saint of missionaries, whom she supported with her prayers. Her feast day is October 1. Pope Francis canonized Thérèse's parents, Louise and Zélie Martin, in 2015.

St. Christopher

According to legend, St. Christopher was named Offerus at birth and lived near a river. Because he was exceedingly tall and strong, he accepted the responsibility of helping travelers cross the river. One day a little boy asked for his assistance. Offerus picked the boy up, put him on his shoulders, and began the journey. With each step, the boy became heavier. Offerus struggled to carry the increasing burden and feared that he would not make it to the other side. When they finally reached the shore, Offerus told the boy that he had never carried anyone so heavy. The child revealed himself to be Jesus Christ, who has borne the weight of the world on His shoulders. At that moment, Offerus's name was changed to Christopher, which means "Christ bearer."

The story of St. Christopher has been labeled folklore, and some question whether he existed. Scholars, however, point to records of the martyr Christopher who died in Lycia (now

St. Christopher, the Christ bearer

ST. ANTHONY'S LOST AND FOUND

"Dear St. Anthony, please come around; something is lost and must be found"[1] is a chant sometimes heard in Catholic homes.

According to legend, St. Anthony had a book of psalms, known as a psalter, that he used for his personal prayer. He also kept his teaching notes in it. One day he couldn't find it, so he prayed that God would help him locate it. Unbeknownst to Anthony, a young novice had taken the psalter and was planning to leave the monastery with it. When Anthony prayed for its return, the novice was struck by a guilty conscience and returned the book to him.

---

[1] Ricardo Liong, "The Saint for Lost Things," Catholic Planet, March 23, 2006, http://www.catholicplanet.com/articles/article137.htm.

Turkey) around the year 251. Christopher's role in carrying the Christ Child across the river led to his title as the patron saint of travelers. Images of St. Christopher can be found on medals, statues, and holy cards with prayers for safe travel.

St. Anthony

St. Anthony, born in Lisbon, Portugal, in 1195, has become known as the patron saint of the lost and found. In 1946, Pope Pius XII declared St. Anthony to be a Doctor of the Universal Church. Statues of St. Anthony usually show him wearing the brown habit of the Franciscan Order, of which he was a member. He holds a lily, representing his purity, and the Christ Child, of whom the saint was said to have had a vision.

Chapter 6

Titles of Mary

Catholics refer to Mary by a variety of names, including the Blessed Mother and Our Lady. Many of these names evoke unique images of Mary.

Titles Associated with Apparitions

Some of Mary's titles refer to her appearances or to other wondrous events in specific locations, such as Knock, Guadalupe, and Fatima. Here are some examples.

Our Lady of the Rosary (also known as Our Lady of Fatima)

Mary's title "Our Lady of the Rosary" dates back to 1571, when Pope Pius V asked all Catholics to pray the Rosary for the victory of Christians over the Ottoman Turks. On October 7, 1571, Philip II of Spain led a Christian group that defeated the Ottomans in the naval battle of Lepanto. Believing that victory was achieved through praying the Rosary, Pope Pius V declared October 7 to be the feast day of Our Lady of Victory. Later, the name of the feast was changed to Our Lady of the Rosary.

Our Lady of the Rosary also refers to the appearance of Mary in Fatima, Portugal, in 1917. On May 13 of

Our Lady of the Rosary, also known as Our Lady of Fatima

that year, three children, Lucia dos Santos and her cousins Francisco and Jacinta Marto, were tending their sheep in a field near Fatima, Portugal, when flashes of light appeared in the sky. The children thought a storm was coming, so they gathered their sheep. As they started walking home, they saw a beautiful lady dressed in white. She told them that she was from heaven and that she wanted them to come to that site on the thirteenth day of each month for six consecutive months. The lady then seemed to drift up into the sky.

After the lady had gone, the children remained in the field for hours and then walked home. Lucia, the oldest, told the younger children not to tell anyone what they had seen. Six-year-old Jacinta, however, couldn't resist announcing that she had met a beautiful lady from heaven.

Soon everyone in town knew that the children had seen a woman who they believed was Mary, the Mother of God. Crowds gathered to watch the children pray in the field on the thirteenth of June and July. Some believed that the children were seeing Mary. Disbelievers complained that the children were creating a nuisance that must be stopped. On August 13, authorities locked the children in the local jail, hoping they would admit that they were lying about seeing visions. The children, however, insisted that they were telling the truth and were released.

The lady appeared to the three children every month from May to October 1917. During her July visit, she promised to perform a miracle so that all would believe.

On October 13, 1917, thousands of people stood in the rain with Lucia, Francisco, and Jacinta as they prayed and waited for the lady to appear. Suddenly Lucia told everyone to put down their umbrellas. Then the sun seemed to spin in the sky and nearly fall to earth. Fearing that the sun would crash into the crowd, people screamed and begged God for mercy. Finally, the sun returned to its normal place in the sky. Everyone's clothes, which had been soaked by the rain, were suddenly dry and clean. The events of that day became known as the Miracle of the Sun.

The lady identified herself as "the Lady of the Rosary"; she is also called Our Lady of Fatima. A shrine has been built on the site of her visits.

Our Lady of Grace

Visit a Catholic school, and you will most likely find a statue of Mary in every classroom. Traditionally, schools have displayed the statue, known as Our Lady of Grace, on a classroom bookshelf with a larger version in the school's hallway or garden.

The title "Our Lady of Grace" stems from Mary's appearance to St. Catherine Labouré in Paris in 1830. It is believed that Mary asked this nun to have a religious medal struck in the image she described. That medal is now called the Miraculous Medal. (See "The Miraculous Medal" in chapter 9.)

Paintings and statues known as Our Lady of Grace replicate Catherine Labouré's description of Mary. According to Catherine, "Mary was dressed in a robe the color of the dawn, high-necked, with plain sleeves. Her head was covered with a white veil, which floated over her shoulders down to her feet. Her feet rested upon a globe, or rather one half of a globe, for that was all that could be seen. Streams of light, representing abundant grace, flowed from her hands."[1]

INVESTIGATING APPARITIONS

Fatima, Lourdes, and Guadalupe are among the many places where people have reported seeing Mary, the Mother of God. Each year thousands say that Mary has appeared to them. How does the Church know whom to believe?

In 1978, the Vatican's Sacred Congregation for the Doctrine of the Faith developed norms so that they could fairly examine each reported vision. The process begins with bishops. When someone reports that Mary has appeared to him, his local bishop assembles a group of experts that includes theologians, medical doctors, and psychologists. This group decides whether the person is of sound mind and body and not seeking financial or personal gains. The group must also make certain that the descriptions of the vision do not contradict the doctrines of the Church. After evaluating the evidence, the bishop has three choices. He can determine (1) that the vision is credible, (2) that the vision should not be believed, or (3) that he needs more help from other Church bodies before making a decision. If a bishop states that a vision is not to be believed, the seer can appeal.

---

[1] "Saint Catherine Labouré and the Miraculous Medal," Our Lady of the Rosary Library, http://www.olrl.org/lives/laboure.shtml.

Our Lady of
Mount Carmel

Our Lady of Mount Carmel

Orders of Carmelite sisters and priests take their name from Mount Carmel, a site in Israel upon which a chapel was built and prayers were offered to honor Mary. On July 16, 1251, Mary is believed to have appeared to St. Simon Stock, a member of the Carmelite Order. She was holding in her hand a brown scapular, a religious article based on the work aprons of monks of the sixth century and worn over the shoulders (see "Scapulars" in chapter 9). Mary offered her protection to anyone who wore the scapular.

Artworks depict Our Lady of Mount Carmel wearing brown garments. She holds the Child Jesus and the scapular in her hands.

Our Lady of Guadalupe

The title "Our Lady of Guadalupe" originated in Mexico. One winter day in 1531, Juan Diego, a member of the Aztec tribe who had converted to Catholicism, was walking in the hills of the Tepeyac Desert near Mexico City when he had a vision of a lady. She asked him to tell the local bishop to build a church on that site. Juan made the request to Bishop Juan de Zumárraga, but the bishop would not act without proof of the vision.

Juan went back to the scene of the vision and once again saw the lady. When he requested proof of her appearance, she told him to climb to the top of the hill and pick flowers for the bishop. Although it was winter, Juan found Castilian roses, which never grew in that area. He gathered the flowers into his cloak and went to find the bishop. When he arrived at the bishop's home, the flowers fell from his cloak, and an image of the lady could be seen on the fabric. That cloak, known as a tilma, is displayed in the Basilica of Our Lady of Guadalupe.

Since its creation in 1531, the tilma has been housed in various churches and has been subjected to poor weather conditions and smoke from the candles of pilgrims. In 1977, scientists used infrared photography and digital enhancement techniques to study the image. They were unable to discern any sketch or outward drawing that a painter would normally use to create an image, and they were unable to determine what method had been used to create it.

In the image, Mary is an adolescent, approximately fifteen years of age, with the complexion of a Mexican girl. Her hands are clasped in prayer, and she stands with the sun at her back, blocking its rays.

Our Lady of
Guadalupe

Our Lady of La Vang

Our Lady of La Vang

Religious persecution in Vietnam escalated in 1748 when the Nguyen Dynasty declared that Catholicism was a sect whose purpose was to overthrow the rulers. Massive attacks against Catholics forced believers to flee to a jungle near Quang Tri. As a group of Catholics hid in the cold, they reported seeing a vision of a beautiful woman holding a child. Recognizing that the woman was Mary, they believed her promise to answer their prayers. They built a small chapel. Later, when the persecution ended, a larger church was built on the site, but that church was destroyed in 1972 during the Vietnam War.

On December 17, 1997, Pope John Paul II acknowledged the Marian vision with a letter to Cardinal Paul Joseph Pham Dinh Tung of Hanoi in preparation for the two hundredth anniversary of the vision of Our Lady of La Vang.

Our Lady of Loreto

The title "Our Lady of Loreto" refers to the stories surrounding the home in which Mary was born and raised and received the message that she was to be the Mother of Jesus.

Around 313, Constantine the Great ordered that a large basilica be built over the site of Mary's home. When turmoil erupted in that area in 1291, Mary's house was said to have been lifted by angels and carried across the Mediterranean Sea to Dalmatia (Croatia). Three years later, it was miraculously moved to Loreto, Italy, where it is believed to have stayed.

Artwork depicting Our Lady of Loreto usually shows either the basilica built by Constantine the Great or Mary's humble home. Because tradition holds that the house of Loreto has been flown across the sea, Our Lady of Loreto is known as the patron of pilots.

Our Lady of Knock

At a time when the people of Ireland faced economic hardships and shortages of food, Mary is said to have appeared to them. On August 21, 1879, fifteen people in the village of Knock, County Mayo, saw a vision of Mary. Artwork referring to Our Lady of Knock is based on the witnesses' testimony that they saw Mary, St. Joseph, and St. John the Evangelist, as well as a lamb and a cross, upon an altar on the side of their village church on that rainy night.

The house of the Blessed Virgin Mary was miraculously carried across the Mediterranean Sea by angels.

Our Lady of La Salette

On September 19, 1846, fifteen-year-old
Melanie Calvat and eleven-year-old
Maximin Giraud reported seeing
Mary in La Salette, a small village in
France. They said that she warned
them of future turmoil and asked
them to pray. Artwork depicting
Our Lady of La Salette is based on
Maximin's description. He said that Mary wore
a crown covered in roses, a white cloak, a bright
yellow apron, and white shoes covered by roses of
many colors. There was a chain around her neck
upon which hung a cross with a hammer and pli-
ers on the crossbar.

The apparition of Our Lady of La Salette was
fully approved by the Holy See on November 16,
1851.

Our Lady of
La Salette

Titles Associated with Images or Religious Orders

Some of Mary's titles are tied to images of her or to religious orders. These titles often reflect attributes of Mary.

Our Lady of Good Counsel

The image of Mary holding Jesus in her left hand with her head bent toward Him is referred to as Our Lady of Good Counsel, or Mother of Good Counsel. This image is often seen in churches and monasteries of the Augustinian Fathers because they have been caretakers of the original painting by this name since 1467.

Our Lady of Perpetual Help

The painting recognized as Our Lady of Perpetual Help has lived a life of intrigue. It is said to have been stolen from a church in Crete and brought to Rome in 1495. Feeling remorseful, the thief asked a friend to give the painting to a church, but the friend kept it. Years later, Mary is said to have appeared to the friend's daughter and asked her to have the painting returned to a church. While speaking to the young girl, Mary called herself "Holy Mary of Perpetual Help." On March 27, 1499, the painting was given to St. Matthew Church in Rome.

In 1798, the French army seized Rome and destroyed St. Matthew Church. Years later, many wondered what had become of the painting. In 1863, Father Michael Marchi, a member of the Redemptorist Order, heard the story and remembered seeing the painting in a private Augustinian Chapel when he was a young boy. When the painting was found there, Pope Pius IX decided that it should be moved to the Chapel of St.

Our Lady of Good Counsel

Alfonso in Rome, the original site of St. Matthew Church. The painting found a permanent home there, where it has been protected by Redemptorist priests and displayed for visitors ever since.

Our Lady of Perpetual Help was painted on a wood panel, approximately seventeen by twenty-one inches. It is Byzantine style in a form known as Hodegetria, which means that Mary's hand points to the Child Jesus as the way to heaven. In the painting, the Archangel Michael is to the left of Mary and the Archangel Gabriel is to the right. Jesus' shoe seems to be falling off as if He has just run back to His Mother. He looks not at His Mother but at the cross held by the archangel.

Our Lady of Czestochowa

The painting known as Our Lady of Czestochowa, estimated to have been created in the thirteenth or fourteenth century, is of Byzantine form and is painted in the Hodegetria style, which means that Mary's hand points to the Child Jesus. It is also known as the Black Madonna.

Although its origin cannot be authenticated, several legends surround the painting of Our Lady of Czestochowa. Tradition holds that the image was painted by St. Luke and that it was found in Jerusalem by St. Helena, who brought it back to Constantinople.

It has been said that when the Tartars were invading Poland circa 1382, the Polish prince St. Ladislaus took possession of the painting and planned to take it to his home in Opala for safekeeping. He traveled to the city of Czestochowa and took the painting to a church on a hill known as Jasna Gora while he rested. The next morning, he packed his wagon for home, but the horses refused to move. St.

Ladislaus took that as a sign that the painting should remain in the town of Czestochowa in that small wooden Church of the Assumption. At times, this painting has been called Our Lady of Jasna Gora after the monastery that has housed it for more than six centuries.

The painting's most unique feature is the scar on Our Lady's face. The legend says that the Hussites stormed the Pauline monastery in 1430, plundering the sanctuary. Among the items stolen was the icon. After putting it in their wagon, the Hussites tried to get away, but their horses refused to move. The Hussites threw the portrait on the ground, and one of the plunderers drew his sword and struck the image twice. When the robber tried to inflict a third strike, he fell to the ground and writhed in agony until he died.

Images of Our Lady of Czestochowa are especially cherished by the Polish community, as it has been linked to many miraculous events in Poland. Pope John Paul II, a native of Poland, expressed special devotion to Our Lady of Czestochowa and visited the shrine in 1979, 1983, and 1991. In her 1966 children's book, *The Kitchen Madonna*, Rumer Godden told the story of a little boy who made a shrine in the image of Our Lady of Czestochowa for the family housekeeper, who missed her homeland.

Our Lady, Untier of Knots

Mary's title "Untier of Knots" (or "Undoer of Knots") comes from the belief that she can undo the knots created by human mistakes. In the sixteenth century, artist Johann Georg Melchior Schmidtner created the image known as Our Lady, Untier of Knots for St. Peter am Perlach Church in Augsburg, Germany. His painting shows Mary untying a long ribbon of knots as the Holy Spirit and angels watch. She stands upon a serpent to undo evil. Mary wears a blue mantle and has twelve stars above her head.

In the 1980s, the future Pope Francis saw the painting while he was studying in Germany. He

Our Lady of Czestochowa

displayed copies of it when he returned to his homeland of Argentina and later gave his predecessor, Pope Benedict, a chalice engraved with the image of Our Lady, Untier of Knots. This image has become associated with Pope Francis and is often used on rosaries and other commemoratives honoring him.

Madonna of the Streets

While Mary is usually clothed in blue gowns and a blue veil, one famous painting, *Madonna of the Streets*, shows Mary wearing more common clothing. The reason for this change of clothing is that the artist did not intend to paint a portrait of Mary.

Around 1897, as he walked the streets of Italy, artist Roberto Ferruzzi saw eleven-year-old Angelina Bovo cradling her baby brother Giovanni in her arms, holding him close to keep them both warm. Ferruzzi approached the young girl and asked her

to pose with her brother for a portrait. The artist named his completed painting *Madonnina*, or *Little Mother*, and entered it in an exhibition in Venice in 1897.

Ferruzzi stated that his work was merely a painting of a young girl cradling a baby.[2] In his mind, the painting did not have religious associations. Admirers of the painting, however, felt that it showed the relationship between Mary and her Son, Jesus. Prints of the painting became popular in Italy. Italian immigrants brought the image to the United States, and it soon became a popular design selling on pins, statues, plaques, and other religious articles in American shops. Upon its arrival in America, the painting was renamed *Madonna of the Streets*. Unaware of the story of Angelina Bovo and her baby brother, Americans assumed that the image was a unique way to portray the vulnerability of Mary and Baby Jesus.

Whatever happened to the model, Angelina Bovo? In 1906, Angelina and her husband, Antonio, moved from Italy to Oakland, California, where their ten children were born. When Antonio died in 1929, Angelina desperately tried to support her large family. Overwhelmed by the stress, she was forced to allow her youngest children to be placed in foster homes and orphanages. Angelina Bovo died in 1972 without ever having told her children that she had posed for the famous painting.

The seventh of Angelina Bovo's ten children, Mary, became a nun with the Order of St. Joseph of Cardondelet and took the name Sister Angela Marie Bovo. Tracing her family's roots in 1984, Sister Angela Marie Bovo traveled to Italy to talk with her mother's sisters. They told her the story of

Madonna of the Streets

---

[2] Barbara E. Stevens, "The True Story Behind 'Madonnina,'" Franciscan Media, https://www.franciscanmedia.org/the-true-story-behind-madonnina/.

the painting. Sister Angela Marie Bovo was able to contact the family of the artist, Roberto Ferruzzi, who gave her his personal notes to document her mother's role in the painting known as *Madonna of the Streets*.

Our Lady of Maryknoll

Images of Our Lady of Maryknoll are often seen on the cards and mailings of the Maryknoll Fathers and Brothers. In 1928, a wealthy Catholic woman told priests of the Maryknoll Order that she would pay for the creation of a sculpture to be named Our Lady of Maryknoll. The only stipulation was that it had to be designed by one of the Maryknoll Sisters. Sister Marie Pierre, a talented artist, accepted the task and sketched a design of Mary holding the Child Jesus. The sketch shows Jesus holding an orb with a cross in His hands. In 1984, Sister Marie Pierre explained, "The orb represents the world. The cross signifies the triumph of our Savior's power over the power of darkness in the world."[3]

Our Lady of Maryknoll

---

[3] Quoted in "Our Lady of Maryknoll," Sr. Marie Pierre Semler, M.M., http://www.sistermariepierre.com/cast.htm.

Chapter 7

Catholicism in the Home

With bedtime prayers, grace before meals, and
family Bibles, the home becomes the ideal place
to nourish the family's faith. "The home is the
first school of Christian life" (CCC 1657).

Crucifixes and Crosses

Step inside a Catholic home, and you may see a cross or a crucifix hanging near the front door. Common practice is to have crosses and crucifixes in the main areas used by the family, such as the living room, the dining room, and bedrooms.

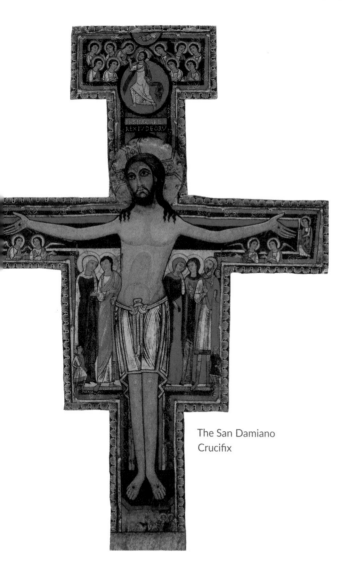

The San Damiano Crucifix

The San Damiano Crucifix

The San Damiano Crucifix is believed to have been created during the twelfth century in Umbria. According to legend, St. Francis prayed before a crucifix of this type in the chapel of San Damiano. Because of its connection with St. Francis, the San Damiano Crucifix is often seen in churches and residences associated with the Franciscan Order.

This icon crucifix contains a figure of Christ and pictures related to His Crucifixion. Those pictures include:

- Mary, the Mother of Christ
- Joseph, the husband of Mary
- Mary Magdalene
- Mary, the mother of James
- The centurion who declared his faith in Jesus
- The Roman soldier who pierced Jesus' side
- The soldier who offered Jesus a sponge soaked in vinegar
- A small rooster (symbol of St. Peter's denial of Jesus)
- Jesus ascending to God the Father

The crossbar directly behind the figure of Christ represents the empty tomb. Angels at either end guard the empty tomb, and surprised apostles stand before it.

The Tau Cross

The Tau Cross, based on the Greek letter *T*, has a simple design with great significance. It is linked to the sign that the Israelites made on their doors with lamb's blood on the night of the Passover in Egypt. The Tau Cross is said to have been one of St. Francis's favorite signs of redemption. Legend holds that St. Francis stretched out his arms and proclaimed to members of his order that their religious garb reflected the shape of the Tau Cross.

The Mariner's Cross

The origin of the Mariner's Cross can be found in Hebrews 6:19: "We have this as a sure and steadfast anchor of the soul." Prior to the year 300, Christians often used an anchor as a symbol of their Faith.

The Mariner's Cross has also been called St. Clement's Cross. Legends state that in A.D. 100, Emperor Trajan exiled Pope Clement to Crimea. Rather than being discouraged, the pope viewed his exile as an opportunity to convert residents of the area to Catholicism. When Trajan learned of the conversions, he ordered soldiers to drown the pope at sea with an anchor tied to his body so that he would never be found. Soldiers obeyed the emperor's command, but there was a surprise: the sea parted, and Pope Clement's body was found and honored by those he had brought to the Faith.

The Celtic Cross

The Celtic Cross is based on the Solar Cross, a symbol of Taranis, a mythological god of the sun. Irish legend holds that St. Patrick combined the pagan Solar Cross with symbols of Christianity as he traveled and preached. The Celtic Cross has become a symbol of faith in Ireland.

THE LOG CRUCIFIX OF ST. JOHN PAUL II

Pope Paul VI commissioned artist Lello Scorzelli to design a crucifix for the papal staff in 1965. Scorzelli's work, known as the log crucifix, became associated with John Paul II because he carried this type of crucifix while he served as pope from 1978 to 2005.

The Christ the Redeemer Cross

Crosses that show a figure of Christ with His hands outstretched are referred to as Christ the Redeemer. The name is derived from the statue of the same name in Rio de Janeiro, Brazil.

In 1851, a Catholic priest, Pedro Maria Boss, suggested that a monument be erected to honor the Faith of the Catholic people of Brazil, but funds were not available. In 1921, members of the Catholic Church secured donations, and construction took place from 1922 until the statue's unveiling in 1931.

Blessings

Blessings can sanctify places and events in the lives of Catholics and prepare them to recieve grace from God.

House Blessing

Enter a Catholic home, and you may see a house-blessing print or plaque hanging above the front door.

Canon law holds that a new home can be blessed only when those who will live in it are present. This is because the blessing is not for the structure but for the family who will reside within its walls. Homes may be blessed by a priest, a deacon, or a layperson following designated rites and prayers. Although a home can be blessed at any time, blessings traditionally occur on the feast of Epiphany.

House-blessing prints and plaques often contain a poem written by Arthur Guiterman (1871–1943). His most famous poem, "A House Blessing," begins:

> God bless the corners of this house,
> And be the lintel blest;
> And bless the hearth and bless the board,
> And bless each place of rest.

Plaques and prints of house blessings have varied throughout the years. In 1941, as war spread across the globe, the Devotional Publishing Company of New York distributed a house blessing that showed Catholic patriotism of World War II. At the top stood an American flag, a cross, and the Vatican flag. The red, white, and blue border, highlighted by stars, surrounded a prayer for the home that stated:

> And bless all those beneath our roof,
> And those who are away.

> Bless the young and bless the old,
> Wherever they may be.

Chalking the Door on Epiphany

Home is the place in which children are cherished, faith is nourished, and visitors are welcomed. Homes are blessed to encourage and strengthen the faith of all who dwell inside.

Many Catholics follow the tradition of chalking their homes on the feast of the Epiphany, traditionally celebrated on January 6 and now often celebrated on the first Sunday after the first Saturday in January. On that day, chalk that has been blessed by a priest is used to write C + M + B above the front door, the porch steps, or an interior part of the home. The letters represent the first initials of the three kings who visited the Christ Child on Epiphany: Caspar, Melchior, and Balthazar. Those letters also signify the Latin phrase *Christus mansionem benedicat*, which means, "May Christ bless the house." The crosses symbolize Christ's Cross.

Although anyone baptized in the Catholic Church can mark a house with chalk, priests often do this for homes within their parishes. For example, priests of St. Stanislaus Kostka Parish in Sayreville, New Jersey, have delighted children by visiting their homes to write the blessing. The clergy of St. Hedwig Parish in Chester, Pennsylvania, have chalked the front door of their church as well as the homes of parishioners.

On the feast of Epiphany, blessed chalk is used to write over the door of the house. The letters call to mind the names of the three kings who visited the Christ Child on Epiphany as well as signify a Latin blessing (photo courtesy of OnePeterFive.com).

Papal Blessings

The *Elemosineria Apostolica*, known as the Office of Papal Charities, helps Catholics obtain blessings from the pope to mark special events. A papal blessing can be represented with a printed certificate or can be on parchment with calligraphy. The document bears a picture of the pope as well as the names of the recipients and the reason for which the blessing has been granted.

Blessing of Food

The Bible contains many examples of persons blessing food and offering prayers before and after meals. For instance, Christ said a prayer and blessed loaves and fishes before feeding a crowd of five thousand people. He prayed before sharing the Last Supper with His apostles on Holy Thursday.

Today, families may ask their priests to bless the food they will eat for holiday dinners, such as Easter and Thanksgiving. Families may take the food to the church or invite priests to visit their homes for the blessing. The food is blessed to thank to God for providing nourishment.

Special Spaces

Decorating spaces in the home with holy articles can draw the family into prayer.

Prayer Corners

Although there is no wrong place to pray, the *Catechism of the Catholic Church* notes that the most appropriate places to pray are personal or family oratories, monasteries, places of pilgrimage, and churches (no. 2696). Catholics are encouraged to set aside space in their homes for prayer. The *Catechism* states, "For personal prayer, this can be a 'prayer corner' with the Sacred Scriptures and icons, in order to be there, in secret, before our Father (see Matt. 6:6). In a Christian family, this kind of little oratory fosters prayer in common" (no. 2691).

Prayer corners in a home show the importance of prayer. A comfortable chair and a table with a Bible and a rosary remind family members to pray throughout the day. Catholic school classrooms also often have prayer corners to encourage children to make prayer a habit.

Kitchen Madonnas

A Kitchen Madonna is a painting, a plaque, or a statue that honors Mary's role as a homemaker. The Kitchen Prayer of the 1950s calls Mary the Queen of Our Kitchen. The Kitchen Madonna plaques of the 1960s showed Mary greeting the Christ Child while holding a loaf of bread, inspiring mothers to nurture their children and make their homes warm, welcoming, and comfortable.

The custom of keeping a picture or statue of Mary in the kitchen has been especially popular in areas near Poland and Ukraine. In the 1966

children's book *The Kitchen Madonna*, a housekeeper from Ukraine tells her British employers that their kitchen feels empty and has no "good place." "In my home, Ukrainian home," said the housekeeper, "we make a good place. A place on top of the cupboard, perhaps, or perhaps on the shelf. Little place but it holy because we keep there, Our Lady and Holy Child."[1]

From 1956 to the 1960s, Enesco Imports produced a series of figurines known as the Prayer Ladies. Sometimes called Mother in the Kitchen, this series included salt and pepper shakers, napkin holders, and spoon rests. The figurines had prayers such as the Lord's Prayer and grace before meals printed on their aprons.

---

[1] Rumer Godden, *The Kitchen Madonna* (New York: Viking Press, 1966), 20.

Seasonal Items

Advent and Christmas items are some of the most beloved Catholic treasures, especially for children.

Advent Wreath

An Advent wreath is often made of evergreens, as a symbol of life, and in a circular form, as a symbol of eternity. It has four candles: three are purple, the color of penance, and one is rose, the color of joy. One purple candle is lit during the first week of Advent, and an additional candle is lit during each of the subsequent weeks, to remind us of the coming of Christ, the Light of the World. The rose candle is lit beginning on the third Sunday of Advent, called Gaudete (Rejoice) Sunday, the midpoint of the Advent season, when we rejoice because Christmas is drawing near. Some Advent wreaths contain a white candle in the center, which is lit on Christmas Eve. Advent wreaths can be found in churches as well as in homes.

Advent Calendar

Catholic children preparing for Christmas turn to their Advent calendars. An Advent calendar does not look like a traditional calendar. It is usually a large picture of a town or a manger scene with twenty-four or twenty-five numbered slots or doors. Beginning on December 1, a child opens one door each day to reveal a picture or a Bible verse.

Gerhard Lang is credited with printing the first commercial Advent calendar around 1908. The custom became popular in the United States when newspapers printed pictures of President Eisenhower and his grandchildren using an Advent calendar in the White House in 1953.

Jesse Tree

How do you decorate your Christmas tree? Do you hang ornaments made by your children and souvenirs of special events? As a Christmas tree might showcase family memories, a Jesse Tree reflects the history of the Faith.

A Jesse Tree is a small tree on which Catholics hang pictures or ornaments that depict key events in salvation history. It is named after Jesse, the father of King David. Isaiah 11:1 states, "There shall come forth a shoot from the stump of Jesse, and a branch shall grow out of his roots." That Old Testament passage refers to the birth of Jesus. The Jesse Tree thus links Old Testament passages that foreshadow the birth of the Savior with the Nativity of Our Lord.

An Advent wreath

St. Francis of Assisi began the tradition of using manger scenes to recall the first Christmas.

Christmas Manger Scenes

Scenes of Christ's birth in a stable have been part of Catholic culture since at least the middle of the fourth century. At that time, the Basilica of St. Mary Major in Rome was constructed with a small oratory built like the cave in Bethlehem. It was St. Francis of Assisi in 1223, however, who inspired the manger scenes that now grace Catholic homes at Christmas.

According to legend, St. Francis walked the streets of Greccio, Italy, in late December 1223 and saw shops filled with glittery Christmas presents. He heard people talk about buying and selling gifts, but nobody spoke of Jesus' birth. St. Francis wanted to do something that would remind the people that Christmas was the celebration of the birth of Jesus. Recalling the religious plays that brought Easter stories to life, he obtained permission from Pope Honorious III to build a religious scene in a cave on the outskirts of the town. St. Francis asked his good friend John Velita to bring animals and hay to the cave. With the animals, hay, and a cave, Francis recreated the scene of Christ's birth in the manger.

Since the 1600s, the Capuchin Fathers, an order of priests inspired by the work of St. Francis, have encouraged Catholics to create manger scenes in their homes. They have been given credit for the popularization of manger scenes in Christian homes.

CHAPTER 8

DEVOTIONAL AIDS

Sometimes tangible items can help deepen Catholics'
spiritual lives. Catholics use statues and holy images
to help them pray, by bringing to mind the holy
persons they represent. Simple elements, such as
holy water and candles, remind Catholics of spiritual
realities, such as Baptism and the light of Christ.

Statues

Many Catholics like to pray in front of statues to give them a visual reminder of the one whose intercession they are asking. Displaying a statue in or oustide a home is also a witness to the Catholic Faith and can remind others to pray.

A St. Francis Statue in the Garden

The Catholic family that enjoys tending to flowers may have in their garden a statue of St. Francis of Assisi. Known as the patron saint of the environment and of animals, St. Francis is often depicted in a garden setting or with birds and other animals.

This association may be due to his "Canticle of the Creatures," in which he praised God's creatures, including Brother Sun and Sister Moon as well as Brothers Wind and Air and Mother Earth.

Statue of St. Francis of Assisi

Mary Statues and Bathtub Madonnas

A statue of Mary on the lawn signals a Catholic home, and travelers on highways and back roads see many. Often the statue stands in a half shell, giving Mary a place of honor. Because the shells resemble cast-iron bathtubs, these lawn shrines have affectionately been called Bathtub Madonnas. In fact, although most of these roadside statues stand in ceramic shells, some actually are encased in discarded bathtubs. These arch or bathtub structures on lawns and gardens are meant to replicate the grotto in France in which St. Bernadette saw Mary.

Fourteen-year-old Bernadette Soubirous was reported to have seen Mary standing in the grotto of Massabielle in Lourdes, France, in 1858. After much investigation, the Catholic Church concluded that Bernadette had actually seen and spoken with the Mother of Jesus.

Since the recognition of Bernadette's vision, churches and schools throughout the world have built their own grottos to house statues of Mary. Father Edward Sorin, founder of the University of Notre Dame, for example, built a replica of the Lourdes grotto on the famous Indiana campus in 1896. The Notre Dame University grotto contains a small piece of stone from the original grotto in Lourdes. Notre Dame alumni fondly recall praying at the grotto during final exam weeks and football weekends.

The Infant of Prague

Catholics recall the infancy and childhood of Christ with manger scenes and stories of the Christ Child in the Temple. One of the most recognizable commemoratives is the Infant of Prague, which shows the Christ Child dressed in the robes of a king.

The original Infant of Prague statue is eighteen inches tall and is made of wax-coated wood. It is believed to have been made in Spain in the sixteenth century. According to legend, Maria Marinquez de Lara purchased the statue in her native Spain and brought it to Prague when she married a Czech nobleman in 1556. In 1587, she gave it to her daughter, Princess Polyxenia of Lobkowitz, on her wedding day. When Princess Polyxenia was widowed in 1628, she gave the statue to the Carmelite Order, and it became known as the Infant of Prague.

As the Thirty Years' War was causing terror throughout Europe, the Carmelites were forced to flee their monastery and leave the statue behind. Returning in 1637, a priest, Father Cyril, found the statue, but it had been severely damaged. After praying, he was able to raise funds to have it repaired.

In modern times, the Infant of Prague statue has been displayed in the Church of Our Lady of Victory in the Lesser Town of Prague. The Carmelite Sisters of the Child Jesus have been responsible for its care. Among their duties has been the periodic changing of the statue's costume. Although most replicas of the Infant of Prague show the figure wearing royal robes of red, the Carmelite Sisters have hundreds of costumes that fit the statue. The nuns periodically change its costume so that it is wearing appropriate attire for the liturgical season or feast day. The entire costume collection is displayed in an onsite museum that is visited by thousands of pilgrims each year and is part of a UNESCO World Heritage site.

Statue of the Infant of Prague

THE SACRED HEART AUTO LEAGUE

A 1955 highway tragedy led to the start of the Sacred Heart Auto League and its practice of giving away plastic dashboard statues.

As more cars began traveling American roads, Father Gregory Bezy, a priest of the Sacred Heart of Jesus, worried about travelers' safety. When his niece and nephew were killed in a traffic accident, he realized that many drivers needed to slow down. He established the Sacred Heart Auto League and asked members to take a pledge to drive prayerfully and carefully.

Father Bezy mailed 4¾-inch plastic statues of the Sacred Heart of Jesus to homes on the mailing list of the Sacred Heart Southern Missions. The Sacred Heart of Jesus statue in a car symbolized membership in this prayerful auto club.

Holy Water and Candles

Holy water and candles engage the senses. They can help prepare the Catholic to pray and can create a prayerful atmosphere.

Holy Water Fonts

Step inside a Catholic home, and you may find a holy water font hanging on the wall near the front door as well as more fonts in the bedrooms. Catholics use holy water to remind them of their Baptism.

Family members and visitors may dip their fingers into a font and make the Sign of the Cross. This practice has its origins in the Old Testament. The great Temple in Jerusalem had fonts of water near the entrances so that the faithful could cleanse themselves before entering for prayer.

St. Charles Borromeo, a civil as well as a canon lawyer, issued guidelines for the construction of holy water fonts when he became bishop of Milan in 1563. "It shall be of marble or of solid stone, neither porous nor with cracks. It shall rest upon a handsomely wrought column and shall not be placed outside of the church but within it and, in so far as possible, to the right of those who enter."[1]

Familiar with holy water fonts in churches, the laity brought them into their homes. Most however, have not been made according to St. Charles's instructions. Holy water fonts for the home range from elaborate ornamental creations of precious materials to plastic fonts and homemade devices. Catholics bring small, clean containers to their churches to obtain holy water to fill these fonts for use at home.

Although early Christians may have had no reluctance to dip their hands into a common church

---

[1] Henri Leclercq, "Holy Water Fonts," *Catholic Encyclopedia*, vol. 7 (New York: Robert Appleton, 1910), http://www.newadvent.org/cathen/07433a.htm.

font, churchgoers of the twenty-first century have a greater understanding of the ways in which germs are spread. In 2009, fifteen people in Italy died after contracting the H1N1 virus (swine flu), so churches in Milan removed holy water from their fonts to prevent the spread of disease. The tradition was restored when Luciano Marabese invented an electronic device that could dispense holy water in a sanitary manner. Similar to an automatic soap dispenser, Marabese's device emitted holy water when a churchgoer passed his hand under the font's motion detector. The first device was installed in a church in the northern town of Fornaci di Briosco. Its use encouraged other town churches to install the devices.[2]

Votive Candles

"Light a candle for me." Christians have used candles to recall Christ's words: "I am the light of the world; he who follows me will not walk in darkness, but will have the light of life" (John 8:12). Churches and outdoor shrines often have candles that the faithful can light as they pray. Catholics praying at home may place candles before religious pictures or statues to create a reverent atmosphere.

Candles attached to religious pictures or statues may be called vigil or votive lights. The term *vigil* comes from the Latin word *vigilia*, which means "watching" or "waiting." When a Catholic lights a vigil candle, he is praying and waiting for news such as a friend's recovery from an illness or the birth of a child. Votive candles are lit when praying for a special favor, such as God's blessing on a new business or academic success. The candles are meant only to inspire prayer and hold no power of their own.

ST. TERESA OF AVILA AND HOLY WATER

In chapter 31 of her autobiography, St. Teresa of Avila says: "From long experience I have learned that there is nothing like holy water to put devils to flight and prevent them from coming back again. They also flee from the cross, but return; so holy water must have great value. For my own part, whenever I take it, my soul feels a particular and most notable consolation. In fact it is quite usual for me to be conscious of a refreshment which I cannot possibly describe, resembling an inward joy which comforts my whole soul. This is not fancy, or something which has happened to me only once; it has happened again and again and I have observed it attentively. It is, let us say, as if someone very hot and thirsty were to drink from a jug of cold water: he would feel the refreshment throughout his body."

2   Eleanor Biles, "Italian Invents an Anti-Swine Flu Holy Water Dispenser," Reuters, November 11, 2009, https://www.reuters.com/article/us-italy-flu-holywater-odd/the-anti-swine-flu-holy-water-dispenser-idUS-TRE5AA3NN20091111.

Holy Cards and Religious Articles

Holy cards, bearing religious images and prayers, have often been distributed by teachers to recognize outstanding work, by pastors to commemorate parish events, and by funeral directors to honor the deceased. Typically four inches long by two and a half inches wide, they may be tucked inside a prayer book, purse, or wallet as reminders to pray.

Holy Cards

The First Holy Cards

It is believed that holy cards first appeared as woodcut prints in the fifteenth century. Such prints enabled those who could not afford more expensive

The first holy cards were woodcut prints from the fifteenth century, such as this one depicting the Crucifixion.

artwork to own pictures of the saints. The invention of the lithography process in 1796 made mass production of holy cards possible. Black-and-white holy cards could be made quickly and cheaply and became readily available. Development of the enhanced process of chromolithography circa 1798 made it possible to print holy cards in color.

Benziger Brothers

The most successful entrepreneurs in the holy-card business were members of the Benziger Family. In 1792, Joseph Charles Benziger began selling religious articles and publishing books in a small shop in Einsiedeln, Switzerland. In 1833, Benziger's sons, Charles and Nicholas, began to manage the business, renamed Benziger Brothers. The brothers decided to print holy cards as well as books. Sensing opportunities in the United States, Charles Benziger left Switzerland to open a branch of the business in New York City in 1853, and Nicholas soon joined him. The family found success. By 1860, the next generation, three sons of Charles and three sons of Nicholas, succeeded their fathers and opened a branch in Cincinnati. An additional branch was opened in Chicago in 1887. The Benziger boys also operated sales wagons that brought Bibles, prayer books, and holy cards to Catholics living in rural areas. The outstanding quality of the Benziger holy cards and religious books was recognized by the Vatican when the Holy See conferred the title "Printers to the Apostolic Holy See" upon the company in 1867. The Benziger Brothers were also known as the publishers of the most famous of Catholic books, the *Baltimore Catechism*. In 1968, Benziger Brothers was acquired by Crowell Collier Macmillan, which later became Macmillan, Inc.

Holy Cards at Funerals

Holy cards distributed at funerals usually bear the name of the deceased, the dates of his birth and death, and a prayer. With the exception of funerals for priests, it has not been customary for Catholics to place a picture of the deceased on a holy card. Families can personalize holy cards, however, by selecting meaningful images, such as a picture of St. Patrick for an Irishman or St. Joseph, the carpenter, for a tradesman.

Holy card collections have revealed trends in Catholic art and thought. The cards of the 1920s had solemn religious images, such as Christ's agony in the garden or the crowning with thorns. Gentle, comforting themes, such as the Good Shepherd or Christ with children, were used in the 1950s and 1960s. Modern interpretations and inspiring thoughts were displayed on holy cards of the 1970s and 1980s. Holy cards of the 1990s and 2000s reminded Catholics of the beauty of nature with photographs of forests, lakes, and sunsets. As each decade has dealt with the trials and triumphs of its time, those thoughts have been reflected in the art of holy cards.

Holy Cards for Devotions or the Causes of Saints

A Catholic may carry a holy card with a picture of the saint for whom he is named or a saint who shares a common interest. Musicians, for example,

Left: This sample of a holy card from a 1912 funeral depicts the Madonna and Child. On the back is an obituary. Right: The Sacred Heart of Jesus has been printed on many holy cards, including this one.

might carry a holy card with an image of St. Cecilia, patron of music. As they leave home for military training, young soldiers might be given holy cards of St. Sebastian, patron of soldiers.

At times, members of the Church may feel that an especially devout person of recent times is worthy of sainthood. Holy cards may be printed with that person's image and a request to pray that he may someday be proclaimed a saint.

Devotional Medals

Medals carried or worn for devotion have a long history in the Church. Christians in the early Church struck medals to remember particular saints or stories from the life of Christ. One example from the second century found in the catacombs bears the portraits of Sts. Peter and Paul.

In the Middle Ages, the use of medals largely waned in popularity. By the twelfth century, the practice of casting tokens in metal grew up around

RELIGIOUS ARTICLES FOR SPACE TRAVEL

Spaceships, the ultimate travel machines, have carried St. Christopher medals above the earth. On June 3, 1965, astronaut Ed White boarded the Gemini 4 spaceship on his way to becoming the first American to walk in space. He took with him a St. Christopher medal, a cross, and a Star of David. When asked why he chose those three religious items, White, a devout Methodist, explained that he could not take an item from every religion in the country, but he could take one from each of the three he was most familiar with.

pilgrimage sites, with the medals serving as souvenirs and reminders of devotion.

The popularity of medals began to grow during the Renaissance but did not reach widespread use until the post-Reformation period. The practice of striking papal jubilee medals began as early as 1475, which helped popularize the idea, as the special medals made their way all around the world.

For more information on specific medals that are popular and are often worn, see chapter 9, "What Catholics Wear."

Religious Medals and Statues for Travel

What's in your car? Do you have a St. Christopher medal on the dashboard or a rosary hanging from the rearview mirror?

Placing religious articles in a car may seem like a harmless act of faith. In some parts of the United States, however, it became illegal to drive with objects hanging from a rearview mirror or sitting on a dashboard because they could block a driver's view of the road. The cherished religious articles of the 1950s could lead to a fine in later years.

Among the most popular subjects for car ornaments have been the Sacred Heart, Mary as Our Lady of the Highway, and St. Christopher as the patron saint of travelers.

CHAPTER 9

WHAT CATHOLICS WEAR

Catholics wear medals, scapulars, veils, and other garments as symbols of their Faith. As Catholics put on these garments and accessories that relate to their lives of prayer, they may remember the words of Colossians 3:12: "Put on then, as God's chosen ones, holy and beloved, compassion, kindness, lowliness, meekness, and patience."

Medals

Perhaps the surest sign of a Catholic is that he wears a medal of his favorite saint or in-dicating a specific devotion.

Patron Saint Medals

Your patron saint can be one who shares your name or your interests. Girls named Teresa might wear medals of St. Teresa of Calcutta or St. Thérèse of Lisieux. Nurses call St. Agatha their patron, and Boy Scout leaders look to St. George for guidance. Catholics wear medals of their patron saints as symbols of their dedication to the saints' ideals.

The practice of wearing patron saint medals dates back to at least 1200. On January 18 of that year, Pope Innocent III wrote a letter granting the canons (clergy engaged in prayer) of Old St. Peter's Basilica the exclusive right to sell medals that he referred to as "signs [made] of lead or pewter impressed with the image of the Apostles Peter and Paul."[1] Pope Innocent III knew that wearing medals would remind Catholics of their Faith.

Medals Recalling Special Events and Patron Saints

Bishops and pastors often issue medals to commemorate special events, such as the establishment of a new parish or the anniversary of a religious organization. These medals may be blessed and sent with holy cards to the faithful. At times, priests sign these holy cards with a cross (+). The cross before or after the signature of a priest symbolizes that he is sending his blessing. It is a custom that began during the days when priests were responsible for large territories and were often too far away to

The Miraculous Medal

bestow blessings in person. One of the most famous persons to use this symbol was John Joseph Hughes, the first archbishop of New York. Archbishop Hughes was called "Dagger John" because he signed his name with a cross, and, more significantly, he was also known as a man who should not be crossed.[2]

The Miraculous Medal

Among the most popular and recognizable of religious articles is the Miraculous Medal. In 1830, twenty-four-year-old Catherine Labouré, a member of the Sisters of Charity, had a vision of the Blessed Mother. Catherine reported that Mary showed her a design and said, "Have a medal made after this model. Great blessings will come to those who wear

---

[1]   Herbert Thurston "Devotional Medals," *Catholic Encyclopedia* (New York: Robert Appleton 1911), http://www.newadvent.org/cathen/10111b.htm.

[2]   Sr. Elizabeth Ann, S.J.W., "Dagger John Hughes," Catholic Heritage Curricula, https://www.chcweb.com/catalog/files/daggerjohn.pdf.

the medal and say often the words that are on it."[3] It took two years to gain approval to produce the medals. Originally called the Immaculate Conception Medal, the name was changed seven years later, when many miracles and acts of goodwill were associated with it.

The front of the Miraculous Medal has a picture of Mary with her foot on a serpent. That image represents triumph over evil. Mary's hands send down rays of blessings. The words "O Mary, conceived without sin, pray for us who have recourse to thee" are printed around the image. The back of the medal has a cross, the letter M (representing Mary), and images of the Heart of Jesus and the Heart of Mary, pierced by a sword in memory of her Son's Crucifixion. There are twelve stars around the images, representing the twelve apostles.

Some antique dealers advertise that they are selling a Miraculous Medal that was made in 1830 or a rosary with an embedded Miraculous Medal that was made in 1830. That, however, cannot be true. The first Miraculous Medals were not made until 1832, and they were not used as the center medals of rosaries until after 1880. Every Miraculous Medal, no matter when it was made, bears the date 1830, the year in which Mary appeared to Catherine Labouré.

St. Benedict Medal

The St. Benedict medal is rich in symbolism. It is unknown when the first St. Benedict medal was struck, but today's most popular medal dates back to 1880, when a newly designed medal was struck at St. Martin Archabbey in Beuron, Germany, to commemorate the fourteen hundredth anniversary of St. Benedict's birth. On the front of the medal is an image of St. Benedict, holding in his right hand a cross—a symbol of evangelization—and in his left hand his *Rule*. On either side of him are depictions

of failed attempts to poison him: a cup of poisoned wine, which broke when St. Benedict made the Sign of the Cross over it, and a raven about to carry off a poisoned loaf of bread. Above these symbols are the words *Crux s. patris Benedicti* (the cross of our holy father Benedict). Around the figure of St. Benedict are the words *Eius in obitu nostro praesentia muniamur!* (May we be strengthened by his presence in the hour of our death!). Below St. Benedict is the date 1880 in roman numerals.

The back of the medal has a large cross on whose arms are the initials of this Latin prayer: *Crux sacra sit mihi lux! Nunquam draco sit mihi dux!* (May the holy cross be my light! May the dragon never be my guide!) Above and below the cross are the letters C S P B, which stand for *Crux Sancti Patris Benedicti* (The cross of our holy father Benedict). At the top is the Benedictine motto *Pax* (peace), and around the circle are the letters V R S N S M V – S M Q L I V B, the initial letters of a prayer of exorcism: *Vade retro Satana! Nunquam suade mihi vana! Sunt mala quae libas. Ipse venena bibas!* (Begone Satan! Never tempt me with your vanities! What you offer me is evil. Drink the poison yourself!) The medal is meant to be used to call down God's blessing and protection, through the intercession of St. Benedict, and to be a reminder to reject all evil and to carry our cross daily and walk in God's ways.

The St. Benedict Medal

---

[3] Leah Kean, *Our Lady's Medal: The Story of the Miraculous Medal* (New York: Guild Press, 1960), 7.

Scapulars

Scapulars are patterned after work aprons worn by monks circa 550. To protect their clothing while working, monks would wear a large piece of fabric, folded in half and with a hole cut in the center so that it could be slipped over the head. Each monastic order had its own colors and symbols. During the Middle Ages, members of the laity sometimes were granted permission to be buried wearing the scapular of the monastic order with which they had become associated. Over the years, smaller scapulars replaced the original apron-sized ones. Wearing a scapular reminds Catholics to live their Faith.

Today's Scapulars

Scapulars are now usually made of two pieces of 2-by-1½-inch woolen fabric attached by two strings. The strings are placed over the shoulders so that one piece of fabric hangs against the chest and the other piece hangs against the back.

Until 1910, all scapulars were made of cloth. On December 16, 1910, Pope Pius X allowed metal scapulars to replace cloth ones but only if one part had an image of the Sacred Heart of Jesus and the other had an image of Mary.

The Brown Scapular

On July 16, 1251, St. Simon Stock, superior general of the Carmelite Order, reported that he had a vision in which the Blessed Mother gave him a Brown Scapular to wear.

Some Brown Scapulars worn today have images of St. Simon Stock and Our Lady of Mt. Carmel. Some bear Mary's promise: "Whosoever dies wearing this scapular shall not suffer eternal fire."

The Green Scapular

In the early 1840s, Sister Justine Bisqu-eyburu, a member of the Daughters of Charity of St. Vincent de Paul, reported that she had visions of Mary holding a scapular. The scapular described by Sister Justine became known as the Green Scapular or the badge of the Immaculate Heart of Mary. It consisted of a small rectangle of green cloth hanging from a green string. On one side was an image of Our Lady, and on the other, her Immaculate Heart, with the inscription "Immaculate Heart of Mary, pray for us, now and at the hour of our death."

The Red Scapular

In 1846, Sister Appoline Andriveau, a Sister of Charity of St. Vincent de Paul, sent word to Pope Pius IX that Jesus had appeared to her many times and showed her a scapular. The pope believed in the apparitions and appointed the Lazarist Order of priests to encourage wearing of the scapular, named the Red Scapular of the Passion of Christ. One side of it shows Jesus on the Cross and the words "Holy Passion of our Lord Jesus Christ, save us"; the other side shows the Sacred Heart of Jesus and the Immaculate Heart of Mary and the words "Sacred Hearts of Jesus and Mary, protect us." Christ promised Sr. Appoline an increase in faith, hope, and charity to those who wear the scapular and meditate on His Passion.

Religious Garments

Whereas medals and scapulars might be worn under outer clothing as a private reminder to the wearer, other articles of clothing, such as nuns' habits or priests' collars, make a public statement of commitment to religious life.

Vestments

When a priest prepares to say Mass, he prays as he puts on the liturgical clothes known as vestments. These vestments are composed of five main articles: the amice, alb, cincture, stole, and chasuble.

The priest begins vesting by placing a rectangular linen cloth called an amice over his shoulders to cover his everyday clothing. The amice represents the "helmet of salvation" (see Eph. 6:17) "that must protect him who wears it from the demon's temptations, especially evil thoughts and desires, during the liturgical celebration." As he puts it on, the priest prays, "Place upon me, O Lord, the helmet of salvation, that I may overcome the assaults of the devil."[4]

The priest next puts on an alb, a long white garment worn by sacred ministers. As he dons this garment, which represents sanctifying grace and purity of heart, he prays, "Make me white, O Lord, and cleanse my heart; that being made white in the Blood of the Lamb I may deserve an eternal reward."[5]

Over the alb, the priest ties a cord known as a cincture around his waist as a belt. The cincture symbolizes self-mastery, and as he puts it on, the priest prays, "Gird me, O Lord, with the cincture of purity, and quench in my heart the fire of concupiscence, that the virtue of continence and chastity may abide in me."[6]

Over his shoulders the priest wears a stole, the badge of his priestly office, a strip of material that is worn for all the sacraments and which matches the color of the liturgical season or feast day. As he puts on the stole, the

A chasuble is typically adorned with holy images, as in this example from the fifteenth century. *Photo © Victoria and Albert Museum, London.*

---

4 Office for the Liturgical Celebrations of the Supreme Pontiff, "Liturgical Vestments and the Vesting Prayers," Vatican website, http://www.vatican.va/news_services/liturgy/details/ns_lit_doc_20100216_vestizione_en.html.

5 Ibid.

6 Ibid.

Nuns' habits differ in style according to their religious orders.

priest prays, "Lord, restore the stole of immortality, which I lost through the collusion of our first parents, and, unworthy as I am to approach Thy sacred mysteries, may I yet gain eternal joy."[7]

The final and most striking garment is the chasuble. The chasuble is sleeveless so that the priest's arms are free to conduct the services. It is usually decorated with symbols, such as the Holy Family or a cross, and reflects the color of the liturgical season or feast day. As he dons the chasuble, which reminds him of the charity of Christ, the priest prays, "O Lord, who has said, 'My yoke is sweet and My burden light,' grant that I may so carry it as to merit Thy grace."[8]

Before vesting, the priest washes his hands to signify that he is moving from the ordinary to the sacred. Vestments remind the priest as well as the congregation of the significance of the Mass.

Nuns' Habits

Many women who belong to religious orders dress uniformly in long, modest dresses and veils. This clothing is known as a habit, which symbolizes consecration, poverty, and membership in a particular religious order.[9] Styles and customs of habits have changed with the times. In the 1950s, Pope Pius XII questioned whether a long flowing habit might hinder a nun's work.[10] The 1965 Vatican II decree

[7]   Ibid.

[8]   Ibid.

[9]   John Paul II, Post-Synodal Apostolic Exhortation *Vita Consecrata* (March 25, 1996), no. 25, http://w2.vatican.va/content/john-paul-ii/en/apost_exhortations/documents/hf_jp-ii_exh_25031996_vita-consecrata.html.

[10]   S. Dwyer-McNulty, *Common Threads: A Cultural History of Clothing in American Catholicism* (Chapel Hill, NC: University of North Carolina Press, 2014), p. 160.

Perfectae Caritatis discussed the practicality of a habit: "It must be in keeping with the requirements of health and it must be suited to the times and place and to the needs of the apostolate. The habits, both of men and of women, which are not in conformity with these norms ought to be changed."[11] Heeding that call for reform, many religious orders modernized their habits, while others no longer required members to wear them.

Pope John Paul II cautioned, however, that habits should not be eliminated. He said in 1996, "Since the habit is a sign of consecration, poverty, and membership in a particular Religious family, I join the Fathers of the Synod in strongly recommending to men and women religious that they wear their proper habit, suitably adapted to the conditions of time and place."[12]

Priests' Collars

Catholic priests are known for wearing the Roman collar, a narrow stiff band of white fabric that is worn at the neck and fastened in the back. The Roman collar makes a man instantly recognizable as a member of the clergy.

When and why should a priest wear the Roman collar? That question has been debated since at least 428, when Pope Celestine rebuked the clergy of Gaul for wearing lavish religious attire that called attention to them. He said that priests should be known "by their doctrine, and not by their dress; by their lifestyle, not by their habit; by the purity of their minds, not by the elegance of their clothing."[13]

Throughout the centuries, the Church has examined the role of religious attire and made adaptations. Nowadays, many priests wear the collar only when they are performing official duties. In order to stop priests from becoming too lax in their dress, the United States Conference of Catholic Bishops examined current practices and issued a statement on clerical attire. Writing for the group in 2009, Rev. Thomas Fucinaro stated:

> The people have a true *right* to the ministrations of a priest, but how can that right be exercised when the priest cannot even be recognized? The significance of the obligation of clerical attire is found first and foremost in the nature and requirements of the priestly life.[14]

Chapel Veils

Until the late 1960s, women did not enter a Catholic church without a hat or a veil. To be prepared for quick church visits, many women carried a chapel veil in a small pouch that fit in a purse. If a woman found herself without a head covering, she conveniently

---

[11] Second Vatican Council, Decree on the Adaptation and Renewal of Religious Life *Perfectae Caritatis* (October 28, 1965), http://www.vatican.va/archive/hist_councils/ii_vatican_council/documents/vat-ii_decree_19651028_perfectae-caritatis_en.html.

[12] John Paul II, *Vita Consecrata*, no. 25.

[13] Celestine I, Ep. II ad Episcopos Provinciae, in *Sacrorum Conciliorum Nova et Amplissima Collectio*, ed. Joannes Mansi, vol. 4 (Graz: Akademische Druck-U. Verlagsanstalt, 1960), p. 465.

[14] Thomas Fucinaro, *Clerical Attire: The Origin of the Obligation: Codicial and Recent Discipline, Governing Legislation from the Conference of Bishops in the United States of America, and Particular Legislation in the United States of America*, Congregation for the Clergy, http://www.clerus.org/clerus/dati/2009-06/16-13/Fucinaro_en.html.

attached a handkerchief or a tissue to her head with bobby pins.

The policies surrounding hats in church were contained in the 1917 *Code of Canon Law*, which stated: "Men, in a church or outside a church, while they are assisting at sacred rites, shall be bareheaded, unless the approved mores of the people or peculiar circumstances of things determine otherwise; women, however, shall have a covered head and be modestly dressed." This canon may have stemmed from the biblical passage of 1 Corinthians 11:4–5, which listed specific ways in which men and women should dress for prayer: "Any man who prays or prophesies with his head covered dishonors his head, but any woman who prays or prophesies with her head unveiled dishonors her head."

In the 1960s, Vatican II brought sweeping change. By the start of the 1970s, most women, especially those in Western countries, stopped wearing hats or veils in church. The new *Code of Canon Law*, promulgated in 1983, did not contain policies on head coverings.

Chapter 10

Religious Art

Through times of war and times of joy, the Catholic Church has sponsored and maintained artistic masterpieces. In the early days of the Church, when many of the faithful could not read, paintings were used to tell Bible stories, teach the basics of the Catholic Church, and to inspire prayer.

Familiar Images of Christ

Many famous images of Christ depict His love, His mercy, and His divinity.

The Sacred Heart Image

When St. Margaret Mary Alacoque was asked to describe the vision she had of Christ's Sacred Heart, she responded, "The Divine Heart was presented to me in a throne of flames, more resplendent than a sun, transparent as crystal, with this adorable

Pompeo Batoni's depiction of the Sacred Heart of Jesus, created in 1760, became a model for others.

wound. And it was surrounded with a crown of thorns, signifying the punctures made in it by our sins."[1]

Inspired by those words, many artists have created images of the Sacred Heart. Pompeo Batoni painted one of the most famous images in 1760. It was displayed in a chapel in the Jesuit Church of the Gesù in Rome and became the model for others. In Batoni's painting, Christ is wearing a red garment as a reminder that He shed his blood for mankind. The blue cape draped over His shoulder represents heaven. He holds His Sacred Heart in His left hand, and His right hand is open and beckons followers to Him.

Depictions of the Sacred Heart can often be found on holy cards, medals, and plaques hung in homes, schools, and churches.

Christ Pantocrator

Artists have portrayed Christ as a baby in the manger and as a man suffering on the Cross. Some of the most inspirational depictions are classified as a Christ Pantocrator, meaning "Christ, All Powerful." This depiction emphasizes the Hypostatic Union of Jesus Christ—that He is both God and man.

The oldest known icon of Christ Pantocrator is found in St. Catherine's Monastery on Mount Sinai in Egypt and is believed to have been created in the sixth century. It was painted with colored beeswax on a wooden panel measuring 84 by 45.5

[1]   "The Most Famous Image of the Sacred Heart," Missionaries of Divine Revelation, http://www.mdrevelation.org/the-most-famous-image-of-the-sacred-heart/.

centimeters. Jesus is shown as a bearded man offering a blessing with His right hand while holding the Gospels in His left.

A careful examination shows that there are subtle differences between the left and right sides of Christ's face. The left side seems to be stern, while the right side has a kinder expression. This contrast emphasizes that Jesus is God and man, a judge as well as the Savior of the world.

Divine Mercy Image

When Jesus appeared to St. Faustina Kowalska in 1931, He was clothed in a white garment, and His hand was raised in blessing. From His heart streamed two large rays, one red and one pale. "The two rays denote Blood and Water," Jesus revealed to St. Faustina. "The pale ray stands for the Water which makes souls righteous. The red ray stands for the Blood which is the life of souls. These two rays issued forth from the depths of My tender mercy when My agonized Heart was opened by a lance on the Cross."[2] Jesus also told St. Faustina: "Paint an image according to the pattern you see, with

2 *Diary*, no. 299.

ICONS

Icon is the Greek word for "image." The elements of iconography as an art form date back to the Byzantine Empire. Icons are known for their simple and stylized — rather than realistic — depictions of Christ, Mary, and the saints. The use of stylization and order is meant to show the timeless and heavenly nature of a moment in earthly history.

Secular paintings have been created by artists. Those who create icons have been called writers rather than painters because their work contains symbols that can be read. Light streaming from heaven indicates God's presence. Large eyes and ears are reminders that the saints depicted focused on God and His Word. Raised hands give blessings. A book in the hand shows that the person depicted could read. Quill pens are included with images of those such as St. Thomas Aquinas, whose writings enhance our understanding of the Catholic Faith.

Christ Pantocrator icon

The most famous painting of the Last Supper was painted by Leonardo da Vinci.

the signature: Jesus, I trust in You. I promise that the soul that will venerate this image will not perish. I also promise victory over [its] enemies already here on earth, especially at the hour of death."[3] Different versions of the image were painted, but Faustina was disappointed that none of them depicted Jesus as beautiful as she saw Him. Jesus consoled her, "Not in the beauty of the color, nor of the brush lies the greatness of this image, but in My grace."[4] The most famous versions of the Divine Mercy image were rendered by Polish painters Eugene Kazimirowski (1934) and Adolf Hyla (1944).

To read more about the Divine Mercy devotion, see "Private Catholic Devotions," chapter 5.

The Last Supper

Catholic homes are likely to have an image of the Last Supper hanging in the dining room or the kitchen. The Last Supper commemorates the final meal Jesus shared with twelve of His followers, His apostles, and the moment when He gave the First Communion (Eucharist) to them. Every Catholic Mass is a celebration of the Eucharist, but the Catholic Church specifically remembers the Last Supper each year on Holy Thursday, the Thursday before Easter Sunday.

The most famous version of the Last Supper, and the one most often found in Catholic homes, was painted by Leonardo da Vinci (1452–1519).

---

[3] Ibid., no. 47–48.
[4] Ibid., no. 313.

Familiar Images of Mary

Many images of the Blessed Virgin Mary are widely known, and some have interesting and miraculous histories as well.

How Mary Is Depicted

According to Reverend Johann Roten of the Marian Library/International Marian Research Institute, the veil and long dress represent Mary's humility and her role as a carpenter's wife. It makes her seem approachable, as one whom anyone could turn to for help. The mantle or cape gives her dignity yet differs from the robes of a priest.[5] In some depictions, as in paintings and statues of Our Lady of La Vang, Mary's cape symbolizes a mother's protection for her children. The cloak of Mary wraps around her children and offers comfort.

While most artists of the 1950s to the 1990s showed Mary wearing light-blue clothing, that shade has not always been the most popular. Earlier paintings and statues portrayed Mary in dark-blue clothes. Reverend Roten says that "Mary's dark blue mantle, from about 500 AD, is of Byzantine origin and is the color of an empress."[6]

Using blue for Mary's clothing has deep theological meaning. First, blue is the color of the people of Israel and those who followed the commands of God. Mary perfectly lived out the call to obedience, so the use of blue is fitting. In addition, in the Old Testament, the Levites were instructed to spread a blue cloth over the Ark of the Covenant. Depicting Mary, the Ark of the New Covenant, in blue, therefore, reminds us of her special role in salvation history.

Mary is often depicted wearing blue, as in Sassoferrato's *Virgin in Prayer*, to signify both that she is a human robed in the divine and that she has a special place in salvation history.

Second, in the Byzantine/Orthodox tradition, blue in iconography represents the divine, while red represents humanity. This is why Mary is often pictured with red clothing covered by blue, and Jesus is often depicted with blue clothing covered by red. This carried over into the Western artistic

---

[5] Rev. Johann Roten, S.M., "Blue, Why Does Mary Wear?" International Marian Research Institute, https://udayton.edu/imri/mary/b/blue-why-does-mary-wear.php.

[6] Ibid.

STATUE OF OUR LADY OF FATIMA

In 1947, sculptor José Thedim received a commission to create a statue to commemorate Mary's appearance to the children of Fatima. Officially known as the International Pilgrim Virgin Statue of Our Lady of Fatima, the statue was blessed in 1947 by the bishop of Leiria, Portugal, in the presence of 150,000 pilgrims to Fatima. At the suggestion of Sister Maria Lucia, it was decided that it would become a pilgrim statue to be exhibited in churches and schools throughout the world. Perhaps its most celebrated journey was its trip to Rome in 1984. At the request of Pope John Paul II, the statue was exhibited in Rome on March 25, 1984, when the pope consecrated the world to the Immaculate Heart of Mary. Sister Maria Lucia attended that event with the pope.

Artwork depicting Our Lady of the Rosary or Our Lady of Fatima is based on Sister Maria Lucia's description of a beautiful lady wearing a gold crown and white robes. Read more on page 58–59.

tradition, as exemplified by Giovanni Battista Salvi da Sassoferrato's *Virgin in Prayer*, among others.

In addition to shades of blue, Mary has sometimes been depicted in garments of white or brown. Usually, the color of her garments has been related to a vision reported to the Catholic Church.

Images Related to Apparitions

Many of the most famous images of the Blessed Virgin Mary are related to her apparitions or her titles. These include Our Lady of Fatima, Our Lady of Guadalupe, and Our Lady of Perpetual Help. To learn more about these images, see chapter 6, "Titles of Mary."

The *Pietà*

Mary's feelings during Christ's Crucifixion could not adequately be described with words, but Michelangelo used his artistic talent to depict those feelings when he sculpted the *Pietà* in 1499.

Michelangelo used Carrara marble to create the *Pietà*, his masterpiece showing Mary holding the dead body of her Son, Jesus. Unlike in other artworks related to the Crucifixion, Mary's face is serene rather than sad to symbolize her acceptance of God's will. The word *pietà* means "pity" in Italian, but Mary's pose is not meant to evoke pity. This sculpture shows Mary as pious, the Latin translation of the word *pieta*. Mary remained pious in her actions, even at the loss of her Son.

The *Pietà* is approximately six feet in length and five feet, nine inches in height. Visitors to the Vatican can see the statue in St. Peter's Basilica.

Triptychs

Artwork in Catholic homes and churches is often displayed in the form of a triptych, a set of three panels with a related theme. The panels are usually joined by hinges, but sometimes they are merely placed side by side. Usually there is a main painting or carving in the center and a complimentary piece on each side.

Triptychs in the Church

Since the Middle Ages, large triptychs have been used as the focal point of an altar. Two of the most famous triptychs can be found in the Cathedral of Our Lady in Antwerp, the largest Gothic church in the Netherlands. Artist Peter Paul Rubens (1577–1640) designed these triptychs for side altars of the cathedral. *The Raising of the Cross* has a center painting of several executioners preparing the cross on which Jesus Christ will die. Each of the two side panels add to the story.

The second triptych, *The Descent from the Cross*, has a theme of carrying Christ. The center panel shows many people taking the body of Christ down from the Cross. The panel to the left shows Mary when she was carrying Christ in her womb. To the right is a panel showing Mary carrying her baby, Jesus Christ, and handing Him to Simeon, the high priest (see Luke 2:28).

Triptychs can be of any religious theme, such as the lives of the saints, the mysteries of the Rosary, or guardian angels.

Triptychs in the Home

Triptychs have long been used outside churches in both the Eastern and Western Christian traditions. Prior to the Middle Ages, triptychs were often used to aid private devotions along with other relics and icons. Today, triptychs approximately six to twelve inches high can still be found in homes, schools, and offices. Many families use triptychs to adorn their prayer spaces (for more information on prayer spaces, see "Special Spaces" in chapter 7).

Triptychs have been used for private devotion since before the Middle Ages, and they can still be found in homes, schools, and offices.

Stained Glass

Stained glass has had a prominant role in Church art and architecture since the Middle Ages. The artistic tradition continues in modern churches, as Catholics embrace the instruction of the Council of Trent, as well as modern Church leaders such as John Paul II, to use art to instruct and to confirm the truths of the Faith.

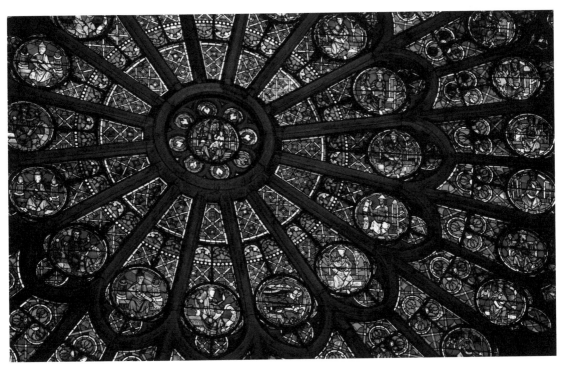

Among the most stunning and famous examples of stained-glass art are the three rose windows at the Cathedral of Notre Dame in Paris. These windows feature scenes from the Old and New Testaments, telling the story of salvation history.

Stained Glass as Art

Stained glass was in limited use in early Christianity, but the rise of Gothic architecture with its large window openings led to a rise in stained glass as an art form. At the time, glass was only in small pieces, necessitating mosaics (small pieces of glass bonded together with lead).

Early stained glass was purely ornamental, but as artists began using figures, it became necessary to paint on the glass to achieve the proper effects. This led to a revolution in the art form as metallic paints were applied and fused to the glass. One of the early adopters of this method was Abbot Suger, the mid-twelfth-century pastor of the Abbey Church of St. Denis, near Paris. He is credited not

STAINED GLASS AS A TEACHING TOOL

During the Middle Ages, the daily life of townspeople often centered on their churches. Realizing that many laypeople could not read, priests and bishops used pictures to tell stories of the Old and New Testaments.

Mary, the Mother of God, is a frequent subject of Catholic stained-glass windows. She is often shown as the Stabat Mater (or "the mother stood") at the foot of the Cross in Crucifixion scenes, scenes from the Rosary, depictions of her apparitions, and more. Other popular subjects include the Sacred Heart, the life of Christ, and beloved saints.

Among the most famous and beautiful of Catholic stained-glass windows are the three rose windows of the Cathedral of Notre Dame in Paris. With scenes from the Old and New Testaments, the rose windows tell the story of the Faith.

only with bringing pictures into his church but with placing that art in colorful window scenes. Abbot Suger believed that light coming through colored glass created a reverent atmosphere, while pictures strengthened faith. Because he was a royal adviser, Abbot Suger's ideas and writings gained attention, and soon after, picture-windows became a standard feature of every church.

France long served as the center of stained-glass art, with the city of Chartres taking the lead. Even now, the windows of Chartres Cathedral are among the most beautiful in the world.

CHAPTER 11

CATHOLIC BOOKS YOU NEED TO KNOW

Before the printing press provided widespread access to
books and education, Catholics learned of the Faith by
listening to stories told by priests and by looking at art in
churches. As books have become more available, the
faithful have turned to the Bible, catechisms, and
missals to gain a greater understanding
of the Catholic Faith.

The Bible

According to *The New St. Joseph Baltimore Catechism*, "The Bible is the written word of God, committed to His Church for the instruction and sanctification of mankind."[1] The Bible is divided into two parts: the Old Testament and the New Testament. The Old Testament describes events that happened before the birth of Christ, and the New Testament tells the story of Christ's time on earth and the work of the apostles.

Do Catholics Read the Bible?

There is a popular misconception that Catholics do not read the Bible. In 1943, however, Pope Pius XII issued the encyclical *Divino Afflante Spiritu* (Inspired by the Holy Spirit), which encouraged Catholics to read the Bible.

Selections from the Old Testament and the New Testament are read at every Mass. If a Catholic attends Mass every day for three years, he will hear selections from every book of the Bible.[2] Since the 1960s, when the Mass began to be celebrated in the vernacular, more people have been able to understand the Bible readings at each Mass.

The Catholic Bible

The Bibles used by Protestants differ from those used by Catholics. Both contain the same twenty-seven books of the New Testament, but Catholic versions contain several additional Old Testament books, called deuterocanonical books: Tobit, Judith, Wisdom, Sirach (also called Ecclesiasticus), Baruch, 1 Maccabees, 2 Maccabees, seven chapters from the book of Esther, and two chapters and a prayer in the book of Daniel. Consequently, Catholic Bibles have forty-six Old Testament books while Protestant Bibles have thirty-nine.

Some Catholic versions of the Bible are the New American Bible (NAB), the Revised Standard Version, Catholic Edition (RSV-CE), the Navarre Bible, and the Douay-Reims. To determine whether a Bible is approved by the Catholic Church, look for an imprimatur in the first pages. The imprimatur is a certification by a bishop that the book is free of errors in Catholic doctrine.

---

[1] Kelley, *The New St. Joseph Baltimore Catechism*, 19.

[2] "Ask a Franciscan: Bible Readings at Mass," Franciscan Media, https://www.franciscanmedia.org/ask-a-franciscan-bible-readings-at-mass/.

Catechisms

While many have come to call any religion textbook a catechism, the true definition was given by Reverend Thomas L. Kinkead in his 1891 book, *An Explanation of the Baltimore Catechism*: "A catechism is any book made up in question-and-answer form."[3]

Catechism of the Catholic Church

Great things sometimes start with a simple idea. In 1985, Pope John Paul II was intrigued when an extraordinary synod of bishops suggested that a manual be developed to put the basic teachings of the Catholic Church in one place. By 1989, a commission of cardinals and bishops appointed by the pope drafted a document and sent it to all the bishops of the world for their input. The final version of this document, the *Catechism of the Catholic Church*, was approved by Pope John Paul II on June 25, 1992.

The *Catechism* is organized in four sections, which Pope John Paul II called the four pillars: the Profession of Faith (what the Church believes), the Celebration of the Christian Mystery (what the Church celebrates), Life in Christ (what the Church lives), and Christian Prayer (what the Church prays).

The *Catechism of the Catholic Church* is a major catechism, one from which less detailed, simpler versions can be derived. It is a reference for adults and was not intended to be used in the religious education of children.

Compendium of the Catechism of the Catholic Church

Sometimes there just isn't enough time to read an entire book. Ten years after he approved the final draft of the *Catechism of the Catholic Church*, Pope John Paul II appointed a commission to condense the material. The result was the *Compendium of the Catechism of the Catholic Church*. This book offers the basics of the Faith in a question-and-answer format. It also has an appendix with basic Catholic prayers and one with the formulas of Catholic doctrine, such as the Spiritual and Corporal Works of Mercy, the Ten Commandments, and the Beatitudes.

Baltimore Catechism

Published in 1885, the *Baltimore Catechism* has become the classic book reflecting Catholic beliefs. It contains a series of questions and answers that students memorize as they make their way through Catholic religious-educational programs.

The *Baltimore Catechism* had its start in 1565, when Pope St. Pius V and the Council of Trent answered Protestant critics by explaining Catholic beliefs in a document known as *The Roman Catechism*. More than three hundred years later, in 1884, the bishops of the United States met in Baltimore to revise *The Roman Catechism* to answer the questions of American Catholics. When the bishops' meeting concluded in 1885, Cardinal Gibbons, head of the American hierarchy, made the new catechism available to churches and schools in the United States. Although it has been most widely known as the *Baltimore Catechism*, its true title is *A Catechism of Christian Doctrine*.

---

[3] Rev. Thomas L. Kinkead, *An Explanation of the Baltimore Catechism* (New York: Benziger Brothers, 1891), 35.

Prayer Books

These books offer a treasury of the rich prayers of the Catholic Church.

Missals

In the days before wholesale production of paperback liturgical guides, Catholics walked to church carrying their missals, books with the prayers of the Mass. The most common was the *St. Joseph Sunday Missal*, the oldest missal still in print in the twenty-first century. Because the Mass was said in Latin prior to 1965, early editions gave Latin-English translations to help the faithful understand the actions of the priest. Catholics could turn to the center pages of the 1957 *St. Joseph Sunday Missal* to find Latin phrases printed in standard black type as well as English translations and directions printed in red type.

The *Saint Pius X Daily Missal*, published in 1956, reflected the initiatives brought by Pope Pius's work known as the Dialogue Mass. The Dialogue Mass enabled the congregation to participate by reciting aloud responses that had formerly been said only by the altar servers.[4]

In 1961, the *Fulton J. Sheen Sunday Missal* became popular due to its easy-to-use features and Archbishop Fulton Sheen's fame as a radio and television personality. This missal printed Latin phrases on the left and the corresponding English translation on the right.

As with many religious articles, the faithful have often struggled to find the most respectful way to dispose of outdated or worn-out missals. In 2012, the United States Bishops' Conference addressed the disposal of religious books by saying, "The Secretariat recommends burying the *Sacramentary* in an appropriate location on church grounds, or perhaps in a parish cemetery if there is one."[5] Following that recommendation, some dioceses, such as Denver, established drop-off locations where Catholics could bring missals that would be buried together in a Catholic cemetery.

The *Raccolta*

The *Raccolta* is a book of prayers, novenas, and pious practices. The first edition was published in 1807. The last edition, published in 1898, has the official title *The New Raccolta: Collection of Prayers and Good Works to Which the Sovereign Pontiffs Have Attached Indulgences*. The 1898 edition of the *Raccolta* was an official publication of the Sacred Congregation of Indulgences and Holy Relics and was published by order of Pope Leo XIII.

---

[4]   Rev. Walter Van De Putte, C.S.Sp., LL.D. *Saint Pius X Daily Missal* (New York: Catholic Book Publishing Co., 1956), 6.

[5]   Zenit, "Disposing of Old Missals and Sacramentaries," posted on EWTN, http://www.ewtn.com/library/liturgy/zlitur392.htm.

ABOUT THE AUTHOR

Dr. Helen Hoffner is a professor at Holy Family University in Philadelphia, Pennsylvania. Her research on the history of the Rosary led her to co-author *The Rosary Collector's Guide*, which provides historical information for rosary collectors, antique dealers, and historians.

Dr. Hoffner is an educational consultant to 20th Century Fox/MGM Home Video and has written several books and journal articles for literacy professionals.

SOPHIA INSTITUTE

Sophia Institute is a nonprofit institution that seeks to nurture the spiritual, moral, and cultural life of souls and to spread the Gospel of Christ in conformity with the authentic teachings of the Roman Catholic Church.

Sophia Institute Press fulfills this mission by offering translations, reprints, and new publications that afford readers a rich source of the enduring wisdom of mankind.

Sophia Institute also operates two popular online Catholic resources: CrisisMagazine.com and CatholicExchange.com.

Crisis Magazine provides insightful cultural analysis that arms readers with the arguments necessary for navigating the ideological and theological minefields of the day. *Catholic Exchange* provides world news from a Catholic perspective as well as daily devotionals and articles that will help you to grow in holiness and live a life consistent with the teachings of the Church.

In 2013, Sophia Institute launched Sophia Institute for Teachers to renew and rebuild Catholic culture through service to Catholic education. With the goal of nurturing the spiritual, moral, and cultural life of souls, and an abiding respect for the role and work of teachers, we strive to provide materials and programs that are at once enlightening to the mind and ennobling to the heart; faithful and complete, as well as useful and practical.

Sophia Institute gratefully recognizes the Solidarity Association for preserving and encouraging the growth of our apostolate over the course of many years. Without their generous and timely support, this book would not be in your hands.

www.SophiaInstitute.com
www.CatholicExchange.com
www.CrisisMagazine.com
www.SophiaInstituteforTeachers.org

Sophia Institute Press® is a registered trademark of Sophia Institute.
Sophia Institute is a tax-exempt institution as defined by the
Internal Revenue Code, Section 501(c)(3). Tax I.D. 22-2548708.